Sacred Hellos

Messages from Heaven

How signs and creativity transformed my decade of mourning into peacefulness and hope.

By: Noelle Rollins

Acknowledgements

This book features my personal experiences with loss, deep grief, and later healing. Without the love and support of my husband, family, and friends, it would not have been possible. I thank them for all they have contributed to my path of healing.

Thank you to the many who submitted stories of their experiences of loss and signs from loved ones, I honor the spirit of integrity and trust in which each story was shared.

This book is not intended as a substitution for therapy or counseling. If you are feeling depressed, hopeless, or unable to move forward please reach out to a grief professional. You will find grief resources at the back of this book.

Cover design, book layout, writing and all artwork by Noelle Rollins
Story submissions from various authors are credited on each page where their stories are shared.
Photo credits: Grandparents holding hands - Pam Dusbabek - Heart of Life Photography
Back Cover photos: Enedina Otanez and Bruce Rollins

ISBN: 9798689772639
Imprint: Independently published

Manufactured in United States of America

Table of Contents

Acknowledgements 5

Introduction...10

What Are Sacred Hellos?..14

Tips to start noticing signs:..15

The Day 18

Feather and Bunny Hellos – Liv Lane..20

One Thing to do After a Death That Nobody Tells You..............................24

The Time My Mom Interfered with Her Own Funeral 28

Losing a Pet..30

The Weeks After...36

Pennies from Marlee May - Josie 40

Dream Visit...42

I Hate Everyone 46

I Believe in Signs from Our Loved Ones After They Have Transitioned - Cheryl.....50

Family - Different Paces and New Faces 54

Talking About Signs with Others 60

Begging for A Sign from Spirit 62

Be Gentle with Yourself 66

The First Big Holidays After 68

Say Her Name..72

Sharing the Same Dream - Christie 76

When We Can't Save Someone 78

Visitors from Heaven During Final Days of Life 84

I am More Than This Partially Broken Me 90

The Grieving Superpower 96

Dream - Nicla 100

You Are Worthy 102

Bee Visitor - Gwen 104

The Path Forward.. 106

Final Thoughts.. 118

Grief Resources... 120

About the Author.. 122

*For my mom, Nancy. You were, and still are,
my greatest teacher and cheerleader.
You taught me what love feels like.
I miss you every day.*

Introduction

If you are reading this book, I am going to assume you have experienced the death of someone you care about. You are not alone. During the deep pain and heartache after a loss it can be hard to be open to signs from spirit. My hope is to broaden your awareness and assist you in your walk-through grief.

I believe we all inherently have the ability connect with loved ones who have passed over. This book will touch on spirit numbers, signs from spirit, and ways to communicate with your angels and loved ones. When I lost my mom, I wanted to understand my feelings and looked for assurances that what I felt was "normal". I studied the stages of grief and signs from spirit while working to integrate that with my own religious and spiritual beliefs. I have written the book I wish I would have had.

This book is not a dictionary of signs from spirit or solely a religious perspective on death. I did not dive extensively into every area of grief, theory, feelings, signs, or how different personality types each handle these things differently. Instead, it is an honest, easy to read collection of stories with lessons from my experiences intermixed with signs, faith, and hope.

Hold close the stories that speak to you in this book and leave the others. Most importantly, if there are people around you who want to rush your grief or do not get your connection to your loved one(s) that is okay. We get you. You are not alone.

Repositioning is a technique I learned to handle grief better. To reposition, we step out of our own story and look at things from another perspective, this book will be an opportunity to practice this technique. Changing perspectives helps unlock our stuck-ness and activates parts of our brain to allow ideas, solutions, and possibilities to flow easier. This helps us handle our grief in new ways.

When we read of others' experiences it can help us to also know that we are not alone. When we can normalize certain parts of the grieving process it helps us avoid using tremendous amounts of emotional energy wondering if what we are going through is normal. This is helpful when we need that energy for putting our lives back together.

Each of us come with a slightly different religious, spiritual, cultural, and internal comfort zone for both the topic of death and signs from heaven. From a Christian perspective you may be wondering if it is okay to talk about signs or communicate with a deceased love one? If you do not feel comfortable talking directly to your deceased loved one, simply pray to Jesus and God to relay messages to your deceased loved one. With that said, I am not here to debate the endless layers of "what's allowed" in each religion, I am here to share my story in good faith. In many areas of this book I refer to options of prayer, meditation, or looking inward. Simply choose what resonates with you. I honor you and your unique path that you are on. I am sending you wishes of strength, clarity, and open-mindedness as you continue in this book. Thank you sharing this space with me.

What to expect

This book is not laid out in chronological order. Grief is ongoing, we all experience it differently and there is no "end". The chapters match that approach.

I am generally an optimistic person, harvesting every life situation for the lessons, while turning pain and heartache into learning and helping others. I have journaled, blogged, painted, cried, sung, talked, and prayed over eleven years of my grief journey; I highly recommend each of those approaches.

I have had a subconscious nudging for years to write this book. I have always considering myself an artist, or even a poet, but never an author until now. Eventually though, I paid attention to the signs, dreams, conversations, and the internal knowing, and I surrendered. I vowed to overcome my fear of what an author is supposed to be. Instead, I chose to show up, write, research, and gather past writings. Mostly, I continue to listen to those around me grieving and their experiences. I have given myself permission to write this book as the artistic poet I am. Perfectly imperfect.

How our brains process grief and healing

All my life I have been obsessed with learning what it means to be aware of our thoughts and emotions. It started when my dad gave me audio tapes of Anthony Robbins that I listened to every night during high school. More recently, I discovered, *Your Brain at Work* by David Rock. This book, especially act II, shares how we can use various techniques to help manage our emotions, including grief. While it is important to feel our emotions, especially in the first weeks and months after a death. There are times where we need tools to hold our emotions together.

One fascinating takeaway from Rock's book was when he explained studies on emotion regulations. When we give the emotion we are feeling a one-word label, such as "denial", "sadness", or "anger" it helps our brain to de-stimulate our distress levels. We often incorrectly assume if we acknowledge a strong emotion by labeling it as "sadness" then it will take over our emotions. Studies by psychologist, James Gross and others show the opposite is true. When we step out of only feeling our emotions and become like a fly on the wall observing the emotions and our reactions to them, we can re-interpret how we see that emotion and name it. We can then create better long-term success in processing our grief.

In addition, Rock explains how further studies show if we suppress our negative emotions (grief), while it may appear on the outside that we are successfully managing everything; inside your brain, the reaction is often an increased release of cortisol (stress) or even elevated blood pressure. Long term suppression of your negative emotions can lead to depression and decreased self-esteem as well as a decrease in positive emotions. Wow, neuroscience is fascinating.

Why does this matter when we are grieving? When our limbic system is overly stimulated it impairs our ability to do other tasks as easily. Could this explain why grief makes it so hard to carry on with regular life activities at times? This gives me hope of why therapy and other solutions can be effective for those with prolonged and paralyzing grief, as well as those looking to effectively manage grief before they reach those levels.

I believe in us

I believe that the world is a better place when we share our gifts, experiences, life lessons, and even our heartaches. We are all learning from one another, and I am grateful for the women (and men) who have stepped into their power and trusted that inner whisper of knowing. Some plowed through the fears, others may have simply tiptoed. By them overcoming fear or doubts and going for their goals they have inspired me to continue uncovering and accomplishing for my own goals. My hope is that I can continue that theme and inspire others. I am figuratively and emotionally standing between the calm and the chaos; bravely finding the path forward that connects truth, trust, connection, and dreams. I invite you to join me. What is your story, your growth areas? What are the areas that have pushed you the furthest, tested you, and forced you to plant yourself deep into the ground, refusing to give up? I want to hear about those areas, learn from you, and be inspired by your perseverance.

During this time of mourning, you may not feel inspired. You may not feel powerful or wise. You may feel shattered and barely hanging on. Read my message above and log it away for when you are ready. There will be a day where you feel the fire swell up inside and you know you are ready to embrace that inner fire. You will learn to hold your grief in a sacred place of your heart, and you will simultaneously rise up and see your strength. You are unique and irreplaceable, and the world is better because you are in it.

What Are Sacred Hellos?

Sacred hellos is the term I created to describe signs we get from spirit. They can also be called God signs, signs from angels, messages from Heaven, God winks. One of those will most likely resonate best with you based on your religion, spiritual beliefs, or other reasons.

Some common signs:

- Repeating numbers; 11:11, 444, 222, or something personal like a birth date, anniversary, or year
- Feathers
- Dragonfly
- Butterfly
- Cardinal
- Blue jay, robin, eagles, or other birds
- Coins
- Dreams
- A song
- Conversations where a message clearly reveals itself
- Bees
- Rainbows
- Hearts
- Lights, orbs
- Electrical (such as a grandfather clock chiming, alarm clock, phone calls from a deceased number)
- License plates (word or numbers that means something personally to you)
- Smells (flowers, loved one's cologne or perfume, cigar smoke, etc.)

You can do an internet search, ask a medium or psychic, pray about them, or trust your knowing if you get one or more of these signs. It is important to know that the sign you get may not be on this list. Each time I have received a Sacred Hello I have felt a knowing throughout my whole body. The feeling is light, pure, and has a high vibration. There is never sadness or low energy around it. Have you ever walked into a room where two people had been arguing? You did not hear the argument but there is heaviness in the air? It feels thick and tense. That is the low energy feeling I am referring to. There are also times where I have found a coin and had no "sign" feeling attached to it. Other times that perfectly placed coin has taken my breath away in awe. It can be fun to research what a sign means, after doing this, take a moment to feel your body's reaction and the confirmation or dismissal of resonance.

Tips to start noticing and understanding signs:

- Slow down. When racing through life, juggling multiple tasks at a time, it can be difficult to notice signs. Approach life with a sense of awe and curiosity; aim to have days with less planned. Instead allow time to notice and be open to magical blessings. This is a healthy approach to life beyond the desire to notice signs. While grieving, we can often avoid our feelings by keeping our minds busy, so slowing down helps in multiple ways. This can be as simple as a few minutes of silence while eating breakfast, taking a walk, during the drive to work, or while falling asleep.
- Feel. Sit in silence and practice awareness. Focus on how your body feels, a certain item in the room, or even imagining yourself being surrounded by a soft color. Do not try to control how things feel, just observe. Simply become aware of what you are feeling, without judgment. This practice can refine your noticing and observing skills, helping you improve awareness in how conversations, events, and your reaction to things feel.
- Ask for signs from your loved ones or pray for signs, then surrender. Do not force signs. For example, if you are desperate for a sign so you head to the bird exhibit at the zoo... then surprise, you find a feather...meh. When you open your car door and a feather is perfectly centered there on the seat; that brings tingles and knowing. Avoid the need to convince yourself or manipulate the settings or outcomes. When I open my phone and it says 11:11, only I know if I was checking it every minute or two for twenty minutes or if I hadn't checked in hours and then opened it to see that number. Do not "sign hunt" to impress others or prove "you're in" with God, Jesus, or the spirit world.
- Be open-minded. If your best friend consistently has a cardinal visitor and she feels a connection to that, do not blind yourself by only focusing on if cardinals are visiting you as well. Go back to the curiosity, the noticing, your signs will be perfect for you.

- Set boundaries. When my son was a baby, I often found myself talking to my mom and asking her for signs that she was around. I was completely comfortable getting a sign... until it was two in the morning and I was walking down the dark hallway to my crying baby's room to feed him. More than once I found myself saying, "but don't give me a sign right now in the dark... it'd freak me out!" My mom always respected that. I think this is part of the reason she comes through in dreams to me so beautifully, she knows this is a way I can embrace the interaction without resistance or human fears.
- We do not get to pick our signs. Each year on my mom's birthday I try to do something special. One year, my sisters and I met up in our hometown and had breakfast at our favorite bagel shop. We got the prime seating on a few comfy chairs with a coffee table in the middle. I brought a deck of angel cards (like Tarot cards with a more positive, angelic focus). The deck was all about messages our loved ones in heaven would like us to know. I let each sister hold the deck near her heart then shuffle. They spread the cards out and let energy guide them towards what card to pick. My youngest sister Alicia was a slightly skeptical, but she played along. The card she drew did not feel like a fit to her. *Hmm*, she thought. We could see frustration and disappointment on her face. Then my other sister went, then me. Then Alicia decided she wanted to ask my mom to guide her to a card and let her pick again. So, she repeated the process of shuffling and drew a card. The SAME card! She could not believe it. She decided to go one more time and yep, picked the same card for the third time in a row. The message was clear, it was up to her to be open to its intention.
- Light and Love. I pray for protection, for love, for only loving and light filled spirits around me. I have no interest in attracting anything negative towards me, so I play it safe. For me personally I am in constant communication with God, my mom, my spirit guides, and angels. In addition to asking for protection I ask them for clarity, to help make the signs clear to me, and to guide me to how best I can use what I know and my life to help others.
- You are the conduit. The same way I get frustrated when churches make people believe that the church is the sole gateway between a person and God, I also think it's easy for us to think that only mediums can connect us to our deceased loved ones. While a medium can be an amazing tool to get clear messages (as can church), you must also honor your own internal knowing and connection to spirit/God. I know many others that have no interest in working with a medium and their comfort level is in prayer. I honor that. Find the scriptures that can support you in your grief and the heavens.

- Signs can be a helpful tool and a way to feel a connection. However, it is important to not put more value on signs, communicating with our loved ones on the other side, and knowing more and more until we lose connection with the lives we are here living. Getting a reading from a medium can be an amazing experience, however if you become too dependent on those messages instead of learning to feel inward, and trust your own knowing then you may be doing a disservice to yourself.

I often think of myself as an "in-betweener"; one foot in the religious, Christian world and one foot in the woo-woo, spiritual world. I believe there are lessons from other religions and the non-religious that we can learn from as well. Each group often uses different terms for similar things. When we bring our walls down and listen to the intention of each other's words we are much more similar than we often realize.

I am fascinated by how different religions and cultures both here in the United States and around the world handle death; including views around burials, ceremonies, rituals, and how we dress the dead for burial. Our attitudes towards death is varying as well. It is often the dreaded end here in American and people have a hard time talking about it. There are other cultures who are much more open about the circle of life and our mortality. It is my dream to travel the world and study these differences.

When we factor in cremation versus burial, somber memorial versus celebration of life, and our relationships with the deceased; we must acknowledge the variety of paths through grief we each experience.

There is no single way to handle grief, a funeral, death, rebuilding after a death of a loved one. Give yourself grace, give those around you grace. It can be easy to judge those who grieve differently than we do. Withholding our judgments can preserve our energy and often our relationships as well.

17

The Day

I picked my phone up off the hotel bed, my eyes were not fully awake after an early evening nap. It was my sister calling. She hurriedly yelled into the phone, "Mom's down! Mom's down!"

"What does that mean?" I asked.

"I think mom died. Let me call you back, I am going to go see. The paramedics are with her." My sister hung up the phone. I sat in the middle of a hotel room nearly 2000 miles from home. I looked up and stared blankly at my husband.

Bruce and I had arrived in Miami, Florida that morning to begin our honeymoon. The day had been a long one, beginning with leaving our house before 3 am back in Minnesota. Our hotel was right on South Beach, it should have felt magical. It did not. It was chilly in the air earlier that afternoon as we strolled the beaches, not the warm vacation weather we were hoping for. Something felt off, we found a coffee shop and hoped it was caffeine we needed. We were ready to embark on a week-long honeymoon cruise beginning the next morning, so we decided to head back to the room, take a nap and refresh. We wrote off the blah feelings to a long morning of travel.

I was still trying to fully wake up as I tried to process these words I had just heard from my sister. I explained to my husband what I knew. I tried to hold out hope for my sweet mom until I knew for sure.

I called back to my parents' house and my younger brother answered. In that moment calmness washed over me as I asked him what happened. He told me my mom had died. They were not sure what had happened. My mom had been complaining of back pain all week, this I knew. I learned that earlier that morning the pain was so bad my dad took her to the emergency room. The doctors sent her home on painkillers with a diagnosis of back spasms.

Late that afternoon she died at home, hours after returning from the hospital. We would later find out she died of undetected pancreatitis. She was only 57 years old.

My husband was already on the phone with airlines lining up flights back home. I eventually hung up with my family and sat there in the deafening and helpless silence. I could not believe it. How could she be gone?

I now look back in hindsight and realize it was no accident that I was out of the state when my mom passed. I often took pride in making sure my siblings were all taken care of. Even when they did not need it, I would try to be strong so I could help them. Same with my dad, I remember once giving him a card in high school apologizing that all my school activities cost them so much money. He would not have it, instead he reaffirmed to me about how happy he and my mom were to be able to provide those things for each of their kids.

I was left to only take care of myself during the 24 hours until I made it back home. I did not need to take care of my daughter, my siblings, my dad, or my grandparents. I had the gift of being sad, being in disbelief, and letting Bruce take care of me. In addition, my brother and sisters were able to redefine their strengths and roles within the family. Both my older brother and I were out of state at the time, leaving the three youngest siblings to take care of things that first day. To no one's surprise, they handled everything great. How they handled things took a weight off my shoulders from that day on, I was able to release myself of the need to take care of everyone. It was a role I'd taken on and taken seriously even though I can look back in hindsight and realize no one had asked me to and they didn't need me to. What a freeing revelation.

I ran as fast as I could to the gate of our second flight that next morning and could overhear my husband pleading for them to wait one more minute, "She just lost her mom", I heard him say as I arrived at the gate, breathless from running. It worked; I made that flight. Eventually, we were in the van of Bruce's sister and her husband. No one knew what to say. Prior to that car ride I figured that someone grieving would be overtaken with grief and all social norms of stoicism would go away. Instead, I found myself a little embarrassed by my inability to control when the tears would flow.

Eventually, we made it to my parents' house. I will never forget seeing my dad slowly walk towards that octagon shaped entryway with his arms outstretched for a hug. He looked half the size of when I had seen him a few days earlier. The brokenness was nearly tangible. We had all lost a best friend that day. How could I be in a world without my mom? That was my first day doing so, the thought of more days to come without her was unbearably heavy.

Feather and Bunny Hellos

If you've read my Signs from Above digital guide, you know I have white feathers around me allll the time and have always considered them a little hello from the angels. But the amount of white feathers in our house has been BONKERS since my dear friend Kelly crossed over in February — on the floor, on tables, on clothes, in our dog LuLu's fur.

Kelly wasn't really into angels, wasn't even sure they existed, but always listened with curiosity & kindness to my stories. Only a few days before she transitioned, not knowing she was so close to leaving this world, she texted me a story about finding a white feather while getting her chemo infusion and how much comfort it brought her. That was so special.

So, to me, it makes sense she'd be pranking me by dropping white feathers everywhere, including yesterday's feather stuck between my cracker and cheese! But then? It's like she wanted to MAKE SURE I knew it was her. Because as soon as I shared the feathery snack on social media, I got up from my chair and noticed a package from my art printer sitting by the front door. I went to open the door and gasped; there was a little bunny sitting on my front step SNIFFING the box! Sniffing it! I ran for my camera.

I cannot see a bunny without thinking of Kelly. As a girl and young adult, she always had pet rabbits; she looooved them. The last one (I think?) she owned was named April Liv. And the last gift I gave Kelly, just because I saw it and it made me think of her, was a pouch for her favorite pens with two sweet bunnies painted on it.

So, to see this little bunny sitting at my front door, inspecting a package of my art, right after I'd told you about the prank I thought Kelly pulled with that cheese-and-feather snack, just felt too perfect to not be another hi from her. And too good and clever not to share with you.

Keep your eyes and minds and hearts open, dear ones. You never know who might be showing up at your door or joining you for a snack, hoping you'll notice they're still right there with you.   ~Liv Lane

**You can find Liv's Signs from Above digital guide at: LivLane.com/signs/*

One Thing to do After a Death That Nobody Tells You

It was November and I was desperately looking through old family photos. It had been 10 months since my mom died and I was missing her like crazy. I found countless perfectly posed photos, pictures of the dogs, random sunsets, and birthday parties. Finally, I found the picture I was looking for. It was the dining room in my parents' home. The photo featured the large dining table fully set for our last family Christmas gathering before my mom would die unexpectedly just weeks later.

What I loved most about the photo, ironically, was not the actual dining table. It was the way my mom hung a wreath in her window or the mirror hanging on the wall that she had faux finished to make it look like the paint was crackling. The photo captured how she hosted, all her personal touches, her showing her love for us for that day.

Take photographs. Go into your loved one's space and take a photo of the way the reading glasses are sitting on the side table, how the spice cabinet looks, or the jacket hanging on the hook. Photograph the wall of framed photos, the collection of ball caps or figurines. Capture the yard, the tools on a workbench in the garage, the view from the kitchen table, even your favorite chair or the kitchen tile.

My dad is more of a minimalist and mourning our mom took up most of his energy that first part of the year. He had very little emotional attachment to the stuff that he and my mom shared. None of it connected him to her. He carried his memories in other ways.

For me however, I see my mom in all of it. I see her hands arranging the flowers into the vase on the table. Her turquoise ring and sterling silver jewelry adorning her fingers and wrists remind me of seeing her hands peeling vegetables before making her famous veggie, pasta salad. These things, especially now that she is gone, trigger loving memories of her. They make me feel connected to my mom's energy and her spirit, her humanness.

In the time after someone passes there is a brief period when the way they had things is still in place. For me having photos is something that I did accidentally. I wish I had done more and had photos of every room. I wish I could remember her lamp, what she was reading, the way her clothes looked all hanging together in the closet.

That November when I was looking through photos, my goal was to put together small albums for each of my siblings filled with images of the houses we all had lived in together. The photos brought reminders of the bold wallpapers, wall hangings, and the way the bamboo plant sat under the stained-glass panel in the trio of kitchen windows. I knew each of us five kids would connect to different parts of each photo.

Take pictures. Even better, do not wait until people die to start taking photos. At your gatherings from now on, do not limit your photo taking to perfectly cropped, smiling faces. Zoom out and capture the room also. The cars in the driveway can also serve as fun reminders of different eras of life. Take pictures of the décor, collections, the people in the stands at the sporting event (not only the athlete). Capture the things that have blended into the background including the people who are not asking or expecting to be the center of attention.

The Time My Mom Interfered with Her Own Funeral

My family and I were together around the clock the week following my mom's death. In this bubble of non-judgment, we were able to jump between sharing memories, anger over her passing, and then flow into the current day's happenings. It was a sacred space for us.

A few days after her passing, we were sitting in the basement of my parents' house. There was a small octagon room under the entryway of the house. The ceiling beams were low; you had to crouch down to walk in there. My dad had put in counters around half the room and converted this area into a sound mixing room for his music. It was in this basement sound room we sat picking out music for my mom's funeral.

My dad found audio from the 1970s and put it on the double reel player. A small group of us listened in silence as my mother's singing voice filled the room. The words started, "He is now to be among you at the calling of your hearts." It was, *There was love* by Noel Paul Stookey. I had never heard my mom sing. My parents had met in the 1970s while my mom was a backup singer and my dad was a guitarist. They shared a love of music. While raising five kids, she gave that up. I could only slightly remember hearing her voice at church. As we continued listening, we all knew; having her voice singing at her funeral was exactly what we needed.

We talked about how my mom would never have allowed us to publicly play a recording of her singing if she were here. She grew more modest the older she was. Then we jokingly said, "Well, she can't stop us now". A weight was lifted as much needed laughter filled the space. It felt so good to laugh. It felt so good to think of my mom as a human with emotions, talents, and vulnerabilities instead of an unfazed, untouchable, angel.

Later that week, we brought the music to the funeral home. We tested to make sure everything worked, and the volume was perfect. As my mom's celebration of life service was underway, everything was going as planned. I sat with Bruce, my siblings, and our kids. Our father, his parents, my mom's mom too, all together in front of us. I held the program in my hand, trying not to curl it up. I was still trying to process what I had just gone through.

Twenty minutes earlier, knowing that the visitation was wrapping up I made my way back up to my mom's casket. I knew they were beginning to usher us to the family room so they could close the casket and begin the service. I stared at my mom's face, memorizing, and studying every feature. Her hands, her rings, her red dress. I could not leave her. My legs would not move. I could not process that this was the last time my body would be next to hers. I reached over and kissed her forehead, trying to lock in this image for me to revisit when needed later. While I know intellectually that her soul was no longer in that body… these were the arms that held me so many times in my life, the face that brought me comfort and love. I had not been prepared for this moment, the leaving her there. It felt as if my heart was being ripped from my body as I tried to rise up to this moment. I worked to regain control of my deep sobs. Slowly I took a deep breath and turned around. Walking away from my mom was the single hardest thing I have done in my life.

Later, as the service progressed, and I noticed her song was about to begin. The silence stretched out, we waited to hear her beautiful voice again. I wanted my grandma to hear her daughter again. I wanted my friends, our relatives to feel her energy through the music. Only, this time, the music did not play. I could tell people were getting nervous, *what was happening*? Seconds continued to tick by... I looked down at my family and said, "She did have the last say, didn't she?" With that we all burst out laughing. It felt so good to sit in the awkwardness of silence and feel her presence surround us.

Eventually, the music came on. It was discovered an outlet had been shut off somewhere. To us, we knew exactly what had happened. My mom showed up to reclaim her voice at her celebration of life ceremony. She came to remind us, *There is love*.

29

Losing a Pet

We adopted our dog Ralphie in 2010, he was a mix of yellow lab and we believe, Collie. We think he was around two when we got him. In the year before he came into our life I'd lost my mom, had an ectopic pregnancy, lost our previous dog Sam, re-took our honeymoon, held a friend's hand during her chemo, and traveled to Texas to introduce my husband Bruce to my daughter Skylar's relatives. It was quite a year. We were ready for some calm and something new and exciting for us all. We found Ralphie online on a rescue site, once we met him it was love at first site.

Over the years as Aspen was born and the kids grew, we eventually moved across the river from Minnesota into our little house on the hill in Wisconsin. Ralphie loved running alongside the jeep through the woods while we collected firewood. He would sit at the top of the driveway on lookout, protecting us from the world. He loved a cool night and a good sunset; he would always appear to be taking it all in. Happy to be alive.

In the fall of 2019, we noticed a few things were changing. Ralphie had lost a lot of weight and he seemed to be ravenously hungry all the time. My fear was that he had gotten into the chicken droppings and developed something from that. Instead, we were given the diagnosis that Ralphie's body was shutting down slowly, he had advanced kidney disease, made worse form the Lyme's Disease he had. We did not know if we had weeks or months but decided to honor him and work diligently at thanking him for being a part of our family for the last nine years.

Within days of the diagnosis Ralphie changed. He laid more, stopped running, and continued to drop weight. We made large blanketed areas for him in the basement by our bed and upstairs on the living room floor. Throughout the week each person took time to lay with him, pet him, and love him.

Looking at this dog who tried so hard to please us, it was heartbreaking to imagine that he could not do all he was used to. If he could, I believe he would have held in any sign of his own pain to make our lives easier.

I have always tended to be more standoffish when it comes to my pets; we had so many growing up that I kept my distance a bit. It was a self-protection sort of thing. With Ralphie though, he had seeped in and gotten my heart. I did not recognize this person I now was. Each day I would sit with him and talk to him and cry, "Ralphie, we are so glad we got to have you be a part of our family.

Thank you for bringing us so much joy. We love you so much and are here to help you. It's okay boy, you did so good. You are such a good boy." Tears would stream down my face; sometimes the words would flow easier than others.

Within a couple weeks Ralphie was barely eating. I would spend the day working and teaching Aspen's homeschool while Ralphie slept. We took little moments of time to spend with him in between other daily tasks. I will never forget one day where Bruce carried Ralphie outside in the morning then carried him back into the living room upstairs before he left for work. I had to go to the workshop out by the garage and told my son Aspen to keep an eye on the dog. Five minutes later I came back inside and noticed Ralphie was not in the living room. It had been a few days since he had walked much on his own, my heart dropped as I went running from room to room trying to find him. Then I eyed the long staircase to the basement. I was scared to look. I was scared he had attempted to walk down and had fallen. Deep breathes... I worked up the nerve and peeked around the doorframe to see the basement. No sign of him. I walked downstairs and looked around. There was Ralphie lying peacefully on the floor by our bed. I will never know how he mustered up the strength to get there.

Ralphie stopped eating within days of that experience. For water he would only take an ice cube here and there. He was fading. He did not appear to be in any pain, so we decided that we would allow him to pass at home. As long as he seemed comfortable, we would do what we could to make that to happen.

Honestly, this was both a beautifully, sacred experience and an in our face, heart wrenching decision. I am glad we were able to make this choice, but I will never judge someone who would have instead taken Ralphie to the vet at this point to have him euthanized. Had I not worked from home, had he shown pain, had Bruce not been able to carry him where we needed... there were so many factors that had one thing been different we would have needed to make the other choice.

Ralphie would still eat ice cubes the next few days, after that he would allow us to wet his lips. By the last couple days, we would sit with a wet washcloth and wet his mouth for him. He mostly slept. He would muster the strength up to change positions. Until the last day he would wag his tail when we entered the room to show he knew we were there, even if he did not lift his head.

A few days before he passed there was a gorgeous winter sunset. We wrapped Ralphie up in his favorite blanket and Bruce carried him outside. We came inside and let him have some time alone outside; it was a beautiful gift to watch him stare off into the sunset that day. It was also a realistic step for us to surrender a bit of control and let him have this experience.

The last few days his muscles twitched more as they released energy. He never appeared to be uncomfortable. The biggest unexpected thing for me during this process was trying to make sure we were doing all we could for him. I would separate this into another category. Having a pet pass away is one thing, and it is devastating. Having a pet die and handling the physical logistics of that process, especially with a large dog, is a different mental and physical feat. Looking Ralphie in the eye day after day, working to understand his needs, while honoring that he was on his own journey was not easy. Actively dying is not easy on a body, and it all was a learning process for me. A trusting process. I worried that Ralphie would walk into the woods on the colder winter days and then change his mind yet be too weak to get back and I would be unable to lift him while Bruce was at work. I worried if he was suffering in any way I was not noticing. Were we making the right choice? Were we being strong or being weak by keeping him with us? Twice I called the vet to talk through how Ralphie was doing and got reassurance from them that they could come out to the house if needed or if we changed our mind to euthanize. All these thoughts ran in a loop through my mind.

In the end I tried to think of everything I had learned and everything that came to me as I prayed for wisdom and calm. What ended up being the strongest and wisest message that I clung to was this, *I can handle this. I can simply hold a space for Ralphie. I can trust that I will know what to do. I can call the vet for assistance, I can do internet searches, and I can call Bruce to come home from work. I can trust that Ralphie has an inner knowing and instincts and I can assist him if I am needed but I can also trust that his body and soul know what to do.*

That final morning, I woke up and spent a few minutes with him as I had each morning before. I set his head on my leg and slowly and gently stroked down his back over and over. I wet his mouth. I thanked him again. I assured him we would be okay and that it was okay for him to go. I told him about my mom and our other pets who were on the other side waiting for him. He put his paw up on my leg that was stretched out in front of me. I put my hand on it and tried to imagine myself energetically exchanging gratitude and love with him. After a few minutes I had to head upstairs to begin homeschooling with Aspen and I told Ralphie I would be back in a little while to check on him.

Around 9:30am I asked Aspen to go peek and see how Ralphie was. Aspen came running back upstairs and said he wanted me to look. Ralphie had managed in his final moments to move off all his blankets and I found him across the room. He laid so peacefully, his back to me. I held my breath as I scanned him and realized he had passed. I tried to be stoic, but I failed. I sobbed as I looked back up at Aspen who waited at the top of the stairs. I mustered up all the strength I could as I walked over to our beloved dog and covered him with his blanket. I felt relief for Ralphie, I knew he was no longer suffering. I felt sadness for us.

Later that day we buried him in a special place on our property. I was grateful to this strong man I was married to. I thought back to the night we found out Ralphie was sick and in his own way of coping, Bruce had gone out to a specific spot near the woods with a shovel and a trailer and started digging. He knew the ground would soon be frozen, so he had thought ahead and dug a large hole and then covered it with plywood and put the trailer of dirt in the workshop. I was grateful again for this physical detail that Bruce had thought of. A way that he felt he could best honor and show love for his dog. We had a small ceremony that evening for Ralphie, we thanked him again and each said things we would remember most about him. I believe it is important to ceremoniously stop time and bring reverence to such moments.

Honoring the dying process for Ralphie was such a sacred, learning experience. There is no rushing death, no planning it out, no outsmarting it. Instead we are left with allowing, honoring, observing. It is up to us to find ways to actively infuse love and gratitude into the sadness and uncertainty. This process strangely enough prepared me for another death that would show up just a few months later in our lives.

I learned another lesson as well during this experience that I had not ever really understood before then. There is a bond that is so deep when we open our home, our embraces, and our daily lives to a pet. There is an energetic exchange that happens. There is a trust they have in us. It is so appropriate to feel they are part of the family. It is so real to feel heartbroken when they pass. In many circumstances it is our pets that we are most open with. They know the realest, unguarded version of us, sometimes they are the only ones who do; yet they unconditionally continue to show up for us.

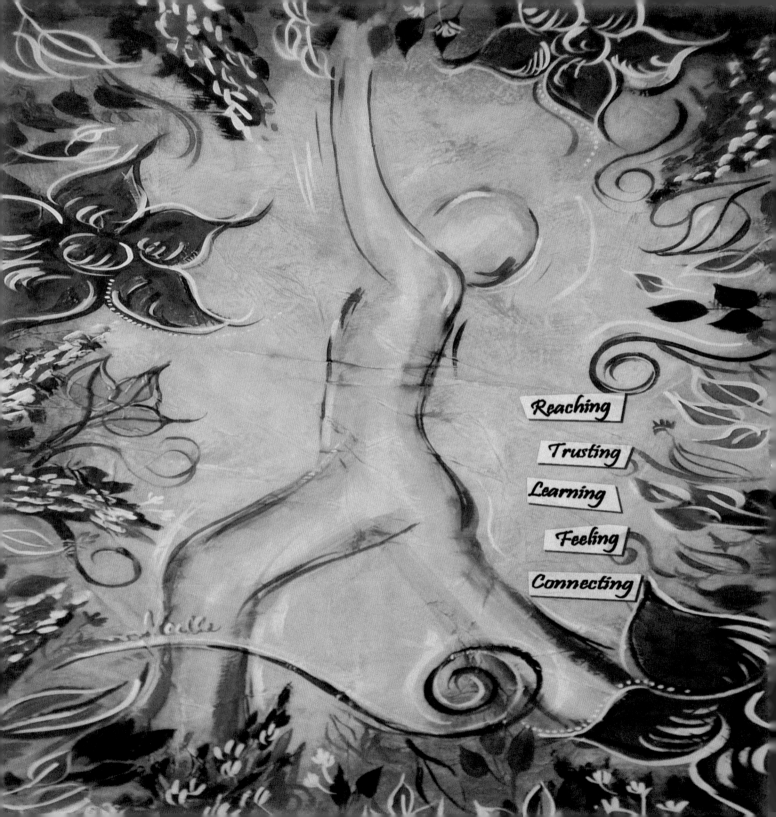

The Weeks After

Three weeks out from my mom's death and I was only beginning to feel its realness. After living across the country in Texas years before, I was used to going months without physically seeing my mom and dad. It took a few weeks for my body to fully comprehend that I would not be seeing her again.

I had to stop treating myself to a daily iced, caramel mocha, I had sunk about a hundred bucks into these drinks over the last few weeks and was noticing my pants getting tighter. I decided I would allow a couple a week. It was one of the only things I looked forward to on the forty-minute drive each morning as I headed to what was my parents' house, but now was only my dad's house.

During this time, I worked as a project coordinator for my dad's company. It was an incredibly fascinating job back when life was normal. We would go into companies and analyze their entire process from when they would get products to when they would ship them. We would write down every keystroke they made on their computers, every time they took their fingers off the keyboard to touch their mouse, every single step. We would write up detailed ways for them to simplify and streamline that process. We would install shipping software and use that to connect their inventory and contact management programs to the shipping company websites. I loved the work and the variety of people.

My dad owned that company, so it was relatively easy for us to take a few weeks off. Our clients were more than understanding. I continued to work part time for him for a few months as we slowly put our lives back together in some way that resembled that of functioning people.

I was also working as an artist; I had a big Valentine's Day show scheduled. In a perfectly orchestrated way from above, the story about me and my upcoming art show ended up in the same printing of the newspaper as my mom's obituary.

There was a protective bubble around me those first couple months. People sent well wishes, but for the most part gave us space. The three-month mark is when I felt things crashing in on me. Clients that had waited to ask questions all came calling and messaging at the same time. Some people around me felt like the three-month mark is long enough and I should be done grieving by then.

I wanted to scream, yet the tears would not stop flowing. How could I be healed and done grieving already? It was only beginning to feel real that this had happened. I was starting to come out of survival mode and feeling glimpses of real life without my mom all around me. I was only 31 years old how could I imagine my life after this without her? I would pick up the phone to call her out of instinct only to remember she was not here.

My daughter was a preteen and needed my focus. Work continued. The world was sympathetic as long as they could be. I was now expected to rejoin society. Only, I was not ready. I felt as if I had a large ball of twine, only instead of twine they were thoughts. It was as if I might be finally be able to get a handle on this ball of thoughts and gauge how big it is if I could just think through my next memory or concern. Only the next memory would not make that ball feel any more measurable. Each thought added a strand to this mental ball that I slowly realized was impossible to contain. I could never fully get my arms around it to understand its size or weight. I thought if I could see how big this ball of thoughts was, then I could form a plan of action. I could regain some control again in my life.

Looking back there was not a specific day that I finally felt like I got a full grasp on this ball of thoughts and feelings... it was more gradual. At some point I felt throughout my body that I could have a memory or feel a moment of wishing she were here, and I did not have to carry that whole ball of feelings along. I could simply let the feeling be as it is. Let it pass through me, thank it, notice it, and keep moving forward.

The thought of a memory simply passing through would have devastated me early on. I did not want to be able to let something move through and leave me. I wanted to sit in the sadness for a bit, sit with her. Sit in a space of stopped time and be with her in my mind. Only, the rest of the world kept moving on. It felt unfair and I did not want to join everyone else in the world that decided things would keep moving.

Thankfully, I was able to continue to carve out a little space to mentally sit in. I was a lucky one. Days after my dear friend gave birth to her first child, her mom died. Her world could not stop, her sweet baby needed her to keep showing up. I hear of people all the time that had a day or two off work, sometimes a week and then had to be back trying to function as if their heart had not been ripped outside of their body.

I worry that there are too many of us walking around that have never been able to heal, instead life had to continue for us. Whether for money reasons or a fear of feeling all those feelings, we have had to jump back into a schedule and carry on. Feelings have a way of coming out and if we do not honor them and heal, too often they control us and will fight their way out at the worst times later in life. It brings me back to what I shared in the introduction; when we suppress our negative emotions long term, internally our bodies are still reacting to the emotions no matter how "together" we appear on the outside. The results are not good and can even limit our future positive emotions as well.

I have a different friend who lost her husband to cancer, a few weeks later she shared that she was going to continue to let herself feel all the sadness but she was going to keep herself tethered to the other side of grief by doing one thing each day that made her happy. In her case she had been grieving on some level for months. Her approach may not fit someone who just experienced an unexpected loss, but it was perfect for her. She honored herself by knowing her life was not over and trusted she would have joy again. She did not force massive amounts of joy; she also did not let sadness swallow her whole.

Finding one thing a day to feel happy about may seem like no big deal to someone who is not in a sad state. However, when the world seems dark and sad it is the bravest thing to set an intention like that. To find a way even in those darkest moments to see happiness in something is so beautiful and strong, she inspired me that day. I have held on to her story, inspired by the idea that we are each different, that we can listen to other people handle grief and learn from them. Ultimately for each of us, it comes down to us trusting our own needs and reaching out how we need to.

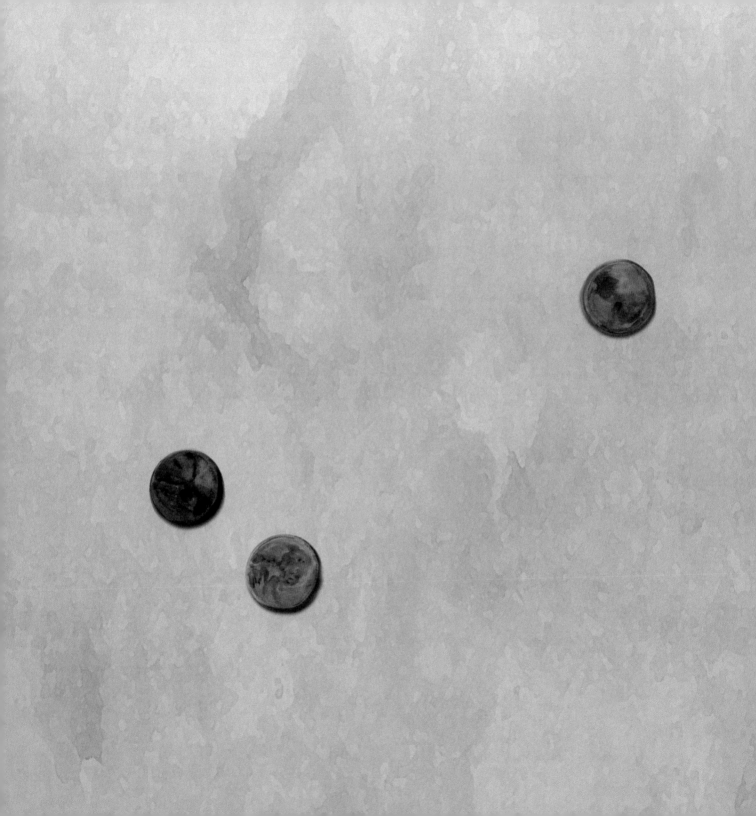

Pennies from Marlee May

My daughter Marlee was just 2.5 years old when she passed away from cancer. When given the terminal diagnosis, they told us she had weeks to months left, but they could not say for sure. We were given just two more beautiful weeks with her.

The night before the funeral, we were setting up the church with pictures and other mementos of Marlee. I went to go grab a bag of photos, sitting in the church pew. When I picked it up, there were two pennies underneath. I had a funny feeling and just knew; Pennies were going to be my sign from Marlee, letting me know she is near.

Days after that, we were looking for a new vehicle. I wanted a dark brown color, my favorite color of vehicle at the time. We found one that fit the description and took it for a drive. I was in the passenger seat and we were cruising along, looking at eagles along the river. Eagles were always a sign from my grandma who had passed. I always pay close attention to them, and there had to have been over twenty of them. I began checking out the car. I looked in the cup holder in the door and there was a penny. I excitedly picked it up. I had gotten a sign from Marlee, just moments after admiring all the eagles, that were "god winks" from my grandma. I don't know what prompted me to do it, but I looked at the date. 1993. The year I was born.

A couple days later, we traveled about 50 miles away to another dealership. There was another vehicle, in my color of choice, which we wanted to drive. As we were going down the road, again, me riding in the passenger's seat, I opened the center console to look at the layout, and sure enough, there was a bright penny. 2015. The year Marlee was born. We bought that car. I never could tell Marlee "No", and I was not about to start now.

Finding change in cars is not uncommon. It is rolling all over my floorboards. This was different though. These were freshly detailed vehicles, not even purchased yet and cleaned by professionals. The chance of finding change twice seems fairly uncommon to me.

Josie Erlandson

Dream Visit

I admit the idea of dream visits from deceased loved was not something I thought about until after my mom passed. Rewind to January 2009, we had been on our honeymoon when my mom died. To get home, we traveled throughout the night and into the morning as we linked together a taxi ride and three flights that eventually got us back to Minneapolis. After spending the evening with family, we made it back home. I was exhausted and glad to be in my own bed.

That night I had a dream. The group of people I was with in the dream turned to the left as we walked through a large room, (imagine part of a hotel ballroom sort of feel). Eventually we turned to our left again at the back of the room and we exited through a set of double doors. Those doors opened to a room full of people. Ahead of me people were hugging, talking, and taking photos together. When I looked straight forward about twenty feet, my mom walked out of a hallway and came towards me. She came face to face with me. Even now, years later I can remember the exact feeling of her face being inches from mine. Slowly she smiled, we energetically poured love into one another as we joyfully looked into one another's eyes. I lifted my hands into a V-shape and gentle cradled her chin and cheeks; holding her face so gently and lovingly as we continued to "fill each other up with love". I can still picture the sparkle of her eyes looking at me, knowing, assuring.

We then turned around and took pictures together, smiling with family and friends. It was a joyous and beautiful experience. I awoke with a deep feeling of peace. Every detail of that dream felt so real, full of love, and good energy. I have carried a peaceful gift from that dream every day since, even throughout the sadness.

Two days after that dream my family was touring the newest, local funeral home; our whole family commented how this place felt like my mom had decorated it. We walked through the area where her funeral was to be held. We started in the front of the room where her casket would be then turned and walked to the back of the room. We turned left and walked out through the rear doors into the lobby. I gasped. It was EXACTLY like my dream. The lobby where all the people had gathered was the same. I looked behind me and the doors matched, in front of me (where people had been taking photos in my dream) was an open sitting and gathering area.

I looked straight ahead about 20 feet. The area where my mom had walked from in my dream... it was the kitchen and serving area of the funeral home. My mom LOVED to cook and entertain, especially in her final years. I had told my whole family about the dream days before, so to then see the funeral home for the first time was such an amazing validation, I was able to instantly show them how the rooms fit my dream.

Over a decade later and I still picture her face in my hands and that look of pure love as she stared at me. I can viscerally feel the unconditional love she and I exchanged.

I have had people ask me over the years about dream visits. From what I know you can tell when a dream is a "visit" when it is clear and vivid. The dream will stick with you and will have an overwhelming feel of knowing or connection. I've had other dreams of my mom in the years since, ones where we were doing activities together, others where I notice her sitting in the kitchen during a family gathering and I struggle to scream in excitement to let everyone know she's there. Those are gifts as well, but most do not carry the same "visit" feeling to me of that first dream. Any time I wake from a dream with her in it I always feel gratitude. Like when we visit with a friend and then come home, that visit and the gifts from it are real even though we are no longer with our friend. The same feeling of gratitude and appreciation can come from a dream, it was time with my version of her, talking, and laughing.

43

I Hate Everyone

I was riding an unexpected high after coming together with my family and having friends show up I had not seen in years for my mom's service, and getting messages from people from all parts of my life. Having that much support was so meaningful. I loved hearing people share their feelings, memories, and offer supportive words. I remember noticing the gratitude I felt for the connection and hugs during the funeral. It was so special to me, even if it was a horrible reason that spurred it on.

The last remnants of adrenaline wore off after a few months. My new reality had sunken in, it all felt too real. Life felt heavy with expectation and society norms that I was not meeting. I could not figure out what my new normal was. Life was now a fun house of mirrors and perspective shifts without the fun. One minute I was handling it all gracefully then next my footing would be shaken, and I would feel off and overwhelmed.

During this same time everything around me felt shallow and fake. Hardly any of what I saw felt like it mattered in comparison to what I had lost and just gone through. Society's constant need for small talk and superficial drama made my skin crawl. I wanted to talk about the meaning of life or what happens when we die. I wanted to talk about the signs I had been getting or talk about our deepest dreams in life and how we planned to make them happen. Life felt short, too short for all the nonsense and time wasting.

Anger filled me. I was not able to access my optimism and patience as I normally had. I wanted to yell at people to leave me alone. Let me be for a while, do not ask or expect anything of me. This was true of family, friends, neighbors, work acquaintances, and clients. Everything felt exhausting and shallow.

This stage did not last long but it was powerful. I have talked with many friends who've experienced loss and have felt the same thing. Some sooner after the funeral, others in year two. Selfish or petty sides of people in can be revealed in tough times, others felt like they were doormats and over-gave without appreciation. In the deepest pain we can look up and realize those we thought would be there for us are not. People do not handle grief like we think they will.

Some stories I have heard involve friends or family of the deceased that could not be bothered during a sickness or before the death but stroll into town as if they had been there all along. People can question and take over with little regard for the person who has been doing their best for a long time and are now exhausted. It is frustrating and can leave us bouncing between devastated, annoyed, and irate.

Create space, say nothing you will regret. Be true to your heart; know that your deceased loved one knows the truth. Act with integrity, give yourself a break. If possibly find a safe person outside of those immediately affected by the death to vent or share your feelings with. Set yourself up for improved healing by surrounding yourself with people you trust.

Certain people showed me a dark and ugly side of themselves, I couldn't ignore it from that point on and our relationships changed. Some have never recovered; others recovered with time.

It is okay to take time and create a healthy buffer between ourselves and the world. There is no need justify your feelings and impatience to everyone. A tight knit group that feels safe and familiar may be helpful to your anger and healing.

I encourage others in this angry and frustrated stage to allow yourself to move through this time without over judging yourself. Feel the feelings but know you are not the feelings. Journaling can also help you gain some perspective and mindfulness about the situation, pulling your thoughts into an observer viewpoint instead of the center of the storm. Apologize to others if needed to clear up past interactions, find books or podcasts that resonate and offer help. Mostly, give yourself grace. Try yoga, art, put together a playlist of music that can pull your mood in the direction you need, talk to a therapist, pastor, or grief counselor.

48

I Believe in Signs from Our Loved Ones
After They Have Transitioned.

I think I always have—even when I was just a child. But as life moves on and with every person I lose in this physical world, my belief in these signs becomes clearer and stronger—absolutely steadfast. And what I've come to realize when a loved one transitions, almost immediately they bring us signs that they are still with us—to soothe us, to ease our pain, to hopefully make their physical leaving just a little bit easier for us. Often, it's within a day or even just a few hours after their passing.

The one person who was the most difficult for me to lose in this lifetime was my Dad. He was my go-to guy for everything, my storyteller, my balance and rock; my feisty, funny goofball. I was his baby, his little girl, his light, his pride and joy. No matter how much I thought I was prepared for his passing, losing someone like my Dad was not easy. He was truly one-of-a-kind—they broke the mold when they made him.

I received the news one morning while I was at work. My Dad had been in hospice for several months and we knew he was getting ready to transition. He and my Mom lived in Nebraska, and I was living in California. I went outside with my cell when my sister called and I sat on the curb while my sister told me that he was gone, and about her and my Mom's last moments with him. I went into autopilot—got my purse and keys, called my husband, and started driving home.

As I was driving home, I noticed out of the corner of my eye a red train engine moving slowly towards me alongside the highway. This was a route that I had driven five days a week for three years, and I had never once noticed train tracks much less an engine. Then it hit me, this was my Dad's first sign to comfort me. Early in his career, he worked for the railroad and his favorite color was red. A crystal-clear sign from him less than two hours after he passed! I think he knew that his sign to me had to be big and obvious to grab my attention for the state of mind I was in.

Once home, I went out back on the deck to sit and breathe and think about my Dad. My husband soon joined me. We sat silently in the sun watching the clouds float overhead in the brilliant blue sky. I closed my eyes for a moment when I heard my husband say, "Look at that, sweetie." I opened my eyes and looked up and there was a huge puffy cumulus cloud in the shape of the letter "M". My Dad's name was Marvin—yet, another sign. I like to think that my Dad was really trying to comfort me in ways he knew I would fully believe came from him. As the months went by after his passing, the signs he sent me were subtle but still clearly from him. His whole adult life, he had been a morning guy. He loved to get up early, go into the kitchen and make a pot of coffee. Then he'd sit at the kitchen table, drinking his coffee, working the crossword puzzles in the daily newspaper and smoking his Marlboros. How I hated the smell of those cigarettes! I remember telling him over and over again, "Dad, I can tolerate just about any cigarette smoke but I just hate the smell of those Marlboros!" One morning, I was up early and had made a pot of coffee (like Father, like daughter). I was sitting at our kitchen table drinking coffee and doing some work on my laptop. Suddenly, the coffee maker started gurgling and sputtering and hissing. I didn't think much of it until suddenly I smelled that signature scent of Marlboros waft by me. I smiled and said, "Hi, Dad. I'm glad you're with me." That happened for many mornings to come.

Then one day on the anniversary of my Dad's passing, I went out in the yard to sit in the sunshine and talk to him. I sat down and suddenly, the words, "Happy Birthday, Dad" came out of my mouth—I'm not sure where those words came from. As soon as I spoke those words, a hummingbird with a bright red (again, my Dad's favorite color) head flew up to my face—about a foot away—and just hovered there looking me straight in the eyes. This was the first hummingbird I'd seen in our yard with a red head, so I knew it was a sign from my Dad. The hummingbird then flew away as quickly as he had shown up. I saw him over at the feeder and asked him to please stay while I went to get my camera to take a picture of him. I went inside, grabbed my camera and came back out—no hummingbird! Then I heard him, turned around and spotted him perched in the neighbor's tree. I asked him to stay there while I took his picture, and he did. I only got two shots before he took off.

While I was pretty certain that this was a sign from my Dad, I was curious about why he would choose a hummingbird as a sign. As far as I knew, his favorite bird was the male (bright red, of course) cardinal. I texted my older sister and asked her if Dad liked hummingbirds. She responded, "Oh my gosh, yes! He loved them. Don't you remember all those hummingbird feeders they had in their yard?" I don't remember the feeders, but I do know with certainty that this was a sign from my Dad letting me know that he is whole and happy and flying free in eternal sunshine.   ~ Cheryl Gibbs

Family - Different Paces and New Faces

Somehow, I thought because I lived much of my life in the same house with my siblings and dad that we would grieve in similar ways. Can I hear you collectively laughing at me? Yes, as you who are reading this already know, I was wrong. My dad, my brothers, my sisters, and I came together in a beautiful way in the weeks following my mom's death. There was a bond formed that we would forever share after grieving the woman we all loved so much. My family was my safe place; a place where all feelings were allowed, and we did not need to put a wall up.

The months following is when our grief splintered off and we found ourselves in different stages. Some of us stayed in the sad stage for a long time, crying randomly for months, and years. For others it shifted to anger quickly, anger and frustration. We felt upset with our mom that she did not get help sooner, we felt furious with her doctors who overlooked major red flags. We felt anger towards our dad that he did not know how sick she was and that he didn't force her to get help sooner. We felt mad at ourselves that we did not see things clearer, speak up more, or somehow know how bad things were. All of this was useless, some unwarranted. Some of us turned to drinking too much to numb ourselves. Some of us slept more than was probably healthy. Some of us shopped and ate and filled the void in ways that really did not fill the void. It was all normal though I am finding out. Not necessarily healthy, but normal.

One thing that surprisingly helped me grieve was the photo of my mom in her casket I'd taken the day before her funeral. I never thought I would be the person who took a photo of someone in a casket. In the days, weeks, and months following her death, that photo of my mom was a gift to me. I looked at it and it helped it seem real to me. I studied her hands, the rings we buried her in, her cheekbones. Somewhere after year 4 or 5 I must have deleted that photo and felt I no longer needed it. I wish I still had it.

As I shared earlier, a few months after she passed, everyone and everything started to annoy me. Nothing mattered as much as what I had gone through. I felt people's judgments over how I handled things as I put together the pieces and how I showed up in the world. I hated it all. I wanted to avoid everyone, every holiday, and every month on the 30th when I counted how many months it had been since her passing. This stage lasted strong for months and came in waves for the first couple years.

Within these previous stages were intermixed times of determination. I wanted to take every lesson from my mom's life; her frustrations, struggles, even her joys, and carry them with me. I wanted to help women like her, I wanted to reach out and dream bigger than she had dared.

I felt as if I was handling it all incredibly well, most of the time. I was showing up each day and trying to stay in "the zone". I was lucky enough to be able to talk through my feelings with friends and siblings, and my husband. I read books, I journaled, and prayed. I asked my mom for support while I talked out loud to her. I reached my arm out a few times on important days and "held her hand" near the passenger seat while I drove. I imagined her being there with me, supporting me, holding my hand back, loving me.

One big area that changed the way I grieved in comparison to my family was that I did not have a newborn baby while grieving that first year like my two sisters did, or a toddler like my brother. I cannot help but wonder how that changes the mourning process. On top of normal grief, both of my sister's bodies were healing and regulating hormones back to their pre-baby selves. This also meant less sleep, and another person to compete for their attention. In contrast, a baby also gave them an extra reason to keep getting out of bed, keep moving forward, and a reminder of the circle of life.

One of the hardest things for my siblings and me was how our dad grieved. He started out appearing strong, we would talk daily, he seemed reluctant but ready for this next part of life. Often, we would meet up for family dinners at a restaurant in our hometown that featured live music and was kid friendly. When I was not working with my dad, other days were spent at his house helping him go through my mom's things. In my mind I had pictured my dad taking this time to work on his hobbies, travel, and visit us all often to hang with his grandkids and us. I imagined us staying connected as we each healed.

Six months after my mom's passing, my dad announced he was going to start dating. How could he love my mom so much for over 33 years and then feel the need to find someone else so quickly after her passing? When I separated myself from my own defense of my mom's memory, I wanted my dad to be happy and feel supported. I went home each night to my husband, I had someone to talk with and share my grief and joy… I hated the idea of him feeling lonely. I would never have asked him not to start dating then, I simply wished he had taken more time for himself and us before bringing someone else into our family dynamic.

That summer at a public park I met his girlfriend for the first time, we will call her Carol. Carol also had five grown children, and she was supportive of my dad and his grieving. The hard part, she was nothing like our mom. At first, she appeared to me as friendly but meek and a bit shy. Weeks later we began noticing that we were rarely allowed over to the house while other siblings and their kids were there. It stressed Carol out to have too many of us together at the same time. This was much the opposite of our mom's attitude of everyone being welcome. This was not easy on us. Eventually it was articulated that Carol had hosted too many events in her previous marriage and was over it. She no longer wanted to host things. We were a gathering family, our dinners and hang out times were valuable to each of us. In the past, the door was always open for any relative or friend to stop by for coffee as well. Things were drastically different after my dad started dating Carol.

My dad's inability to set proper boundaries made this transition harder. I will never forget one particular day that first fall when my sisters and I agreed to go through boxes in his house. He did not want to go through anything himself so he asked us to make decisions on what stayed, what would be divided between us kids, and what would be donated. We went through family ornaments, serving dishes, and holiday decor that brought endless memories; sorting and deciding along the way. At some point my dad sent his girlfriend downstairs to where we were working and requested that we begin asking his girlfriend if she wanted to keep anything for "their" house before we could take it. I will never forget sitting in the basement, racks of things my mom had bought or used for our family holiday traditions in the boxes in front of us and having this strangers presence in this incredibly difficult and complicated moment.

Carol had her own lifetime of holiday décor, her and my dad had only been dating for 4 months at that point; it felt like a dishonor to our bond with our mom to be forced to ask a virtual stranger to decide these things. Of course, they were my dad's things. He could do whatever he wished with them, including not give us any. The frustration came, I believe, from him making Carol the gatekeeper. The decider. Looking back, we should have called a timeout; we should have pulled our dad aside and made it clear that he had just put his new girlfriend and us in an incredibly awkward position. This was not her doing, this was on my dad. He was trying to give her a chance to see what she liked and maybe also to have us all bond. Instead, he was throwing her to the wolves essentially. We resented this; we were the wolves. We were polite and full of begrudging Minnesota "nice", but wolves, nonetheless.

My parents raised kids with strong personalities that Carol was now finding herself at passive aggressive odds with. The first heartbreaking Thanksgiving, then Christmas passed, my dad did not host any more holidays. It was frustrating and sad. Traditions were already changed so much by not having our mom there, now we had lost our family gathering traditions as well. More than that, we felt we were losing our dad a bit too. At the time it felt as if we were being wiped out of our dad's life as a

revisionist history was being created about our lives prior to Carol. This transition was not easy. Each of us kids handled it very differently.

The difficulties continued with my dad's directing of Carol to make herself at home. As she and my dad redecorated the house, we watched pieces of our mom and lives wiped away one room at a time. Intellectually this was understandable, emotionally it took more work.

Eleven years later, my dad is still with Carol. While I still selfishly wish she were a bit more open and inclusive, I can see now that my dad got to live 33+ years with my mom and her style of living. He raised kids with her, built his career with her, loved her, shared laughs with her, attended endless activities of their kids together... this was his time now to live for him. A time for something different.

My dad was getting a second chapter. A new set of circumstances to choose someone to spend his days with. Yes, I still wish they would host family gatherings. Yes, as I see them spend weeks at a time with her children and grandchildren, I do find myself a bit jealous. While my mom was alive my dad got to know his oldest two grandchildren so well, they adored him; most his grandchildren born over the last decade have not gotten to know that side of him. Grief broke him apart. We had a very idyllic childhood, he was an amazing dad to have growing up, we get glimpses of that "old dad" side of him more and more as each year passes.

Through lots of emotional work and learning I have come to realize that my dad is holding his own pain. He is imperfectly trying to find his way forward. The reality is, he's not that different than when my mom was alive; he supported her plans then the same as he supports Carol's now. The difference is that our mom's devotion was to us and Carol's devotion is to her children.

I wish he were more independent and would have taken more time to set up his life again how he wanted it and then find someone to match that life. The more I talk with others though the more I realize how rare this would have been. I share all this, not because my dad is a bad guy. He is human, and the frustrations I shared above are incredibly common between a child and parent after the other parent passes. I share them so you know you are not alone if you have had a hard time welcoming a new member into your family dynamic. All that I shared above has evolved over more than a decade. Missing in that story is long stretches of wishing for old times, old traditions. Finding a new balance of our role as adult kids, where to we step in and where do we need to step back.

A friend of mine, Bridgette shared with me so eloquently the other side of this story last year. She was "Carol" in her husband's kid's eyes. His kids too are full grown; they too have never gotten to know all she has to offer. It is taken her years to slowly nurture those relationships. She explained the absolute heartbreak it is to support a man who lost his wife while also being seen as the villain. To see the man she has fallen in love with broken and trying to find any semblance of happiness again is not easy. There are parts of life that a child's love cannot fill; my dad, and Bridgette's husband, deserve to have filled. It was such a gift to talk with her and see things from her (and Carol's) perspective. All the wasted hours of anger or what ifs. Really, it is about learning to speak up, learning to articulate concerns and learning to respect that most people are doing the best they can.

As a family, after 11 years we have had years we each had to hypothetically put on our own oxygen masks and get our lives in order and years where we were a bit codependent with each other and needed deeper levels of support. I believe we have now found a healthy respect for how different each of our life partners, kids, and life choices are. Family therapy would have helped things get here sooner I imagine, but I am grateful for where we are now.

Things are messy and hard after one person in a family is suddenly removed. In the years since my own mom's passing, I have heard numerous stories from others about family, anger, theft, and blame after someone passes. Horrible situations. If you have experienced these, my heart goes out to you. Whether you had to pursue legal action, bow out, find peace by cutting out destructive relations, or must handle everything yourself. Reach out, find support. There are online support groups, in person grief groups, support after loss social media groups, legal counsel, pastors, and therapists. Read about setting boundaries; get advice before being guilted into handing over money or property. You do not have to face this alone. You will get through this. Just keep going. Keep waking up and taking things one day, one hour at a time.

Talking About Signs with Others

Are you hesitant to talk about the signs you have been getting? It can feel incredibly vulnerable to share a story about something this personal. I remember confiding in others about how the same song kept coming on or how I would keep seeing 11:11 all the time. They would say, "well I'm sure it's just coincidence," or "you probably are wanting to see the number, so you keep looking until you see it." In theory they could be right.

In my deepest knowing though... I knew it was more than that. I felt an energy shift and would get chills when I would hear a certain song or see other signs. I would have been giving my internal certainty over to the judgment of others had I depended on their validation. Trust yourself. It does not matter if ANYONE else believes you. Do not look for signs with the intention of telling others. Instead simply allow yourself to be aware. I imagine spirit working so hard to get our attention and we have our heads down, on our phones, or blocked in a literal place too often. Things are happening if we take notice.

When I did get feedback from people that went against my experience, I would remember to never discuss it with them again. Part of my response was out of respect for them and their beliefs. I did not want to ever have them feel like I was pressuring them to believe something that did not feel right to them. Secondly, I chose not to talk about it with doubters simply to protect my own energy. I did not need to spend any of my energy playing defense for something I felt so strongly. Especially with those who had not experienced the death of someone close to them. I have seen too many situations where people flippantly make comments doubting things they have never contemplated. Time passes or they experience a loss and a shift happens, suddenly they get it. Life opened their eyes and hearts when the time was right, without me spending my precious energy "convincing" them.

After getting a closed minded response, rather than feel frustrated I would often re-frame it in my mind, *I've planted a seed and when they are ready or down the road if they ever get a sign, then maybe I created an opening in their beliefs so that they would notice it.* You can trust your knowing. You do not need validation from others. It is between you and your heart. Savor it.

Begging for A Sign from Spirit

One of the hardest things I have found after someone passes is wanting to know they are okay. We miss them, we ache for them. We want to know they are still connected to us in some way.

I remember sharing my dream with my family and then months later having a very clear 2nd dream visit as well. My sister told me had been wishing for a dream visit too and had never had one.

Why do some of us remember dreams better than others? Maybe my sister or others have had a dream visit but aren't in the habit on remembering dreams? I also recently heard a sleep scientist say that those of us who do not wake up to an alarm clock or instant interruptions tend to be better at remembering our dreams. We can stay in our dream state a bit longer and wake up and think about the dream or subconsciously process it before jumping out of bed and beginning our day. I'd like to think that in the big picture where time doesn't matter as much, we each receive the confirmations we are needing when we need them for our highest good, not simply when we want them. This can be dreams or signs in general.

After my mom died in early 2009, her death was unexpected so along with the grieving there was also an incredible amount of shock. There was a tangible feeling of deep loss not having our mom with us as my siblings and I continued to have more babies, get married, and make more life changes. Most of us have felt her around at different times; we have gotten signs or had dreams. As you know though, there is nothing like the direct hug, conversation, or looking into our loved one's eyes.

I have always been skeptical of people who say they can communicate with spirit. Not skeptical that mediumship is possible, I have friends who can consciously do this. I do not necessarily believe every medium or psychic, nor do I trust all their intentions. To be fair, I also have this distrust of churches as well. I do not trust many of their agendas. People are messy and our greed and egos can mess up even the most beautiful of intentions.

A couple years after my mom died, I had a call with a medium. She later mailed me a CD recording of our call. I was grateful for this because during the call I was guarded, as much as I tried to remember everything from our session by memory, there were things I had forgotten until I listed to the recording.

During the call, the medium very clearly and specifically talked about things that had happened that day. She talked about what my husband had said to me right before the call. She also passed along my mom's motherly guidance based on what my sister and I had talked about the night before the call. (I had never mentioned our conversation to her). When I asked about messages for my brothers or dad the next three things she talked about were for my brothers and then my dad. It was unbelievable. I loved too that during the call there were a couple things I did not understand. For instance, she said my mom was showing her a strand of pearls. Yes, I had a pearl necklace of my mom's, but it was not particularly a favorite of mine or sentimental to me, so I did not feel like that was a fit for what I was being told. The medium told me to keep it in mind and I will know it's meaning down the road.

The next morning, I was sitting having coffee and I looked down at my mug and gasped... the mug was from my honeymoon cruise. The cruise I was hours from boarding when I found out my mom had passed away, the Norwegian Pearl. Along the side of the ship was a gigantic image of a strand of pearls. This is the same ship that we re-took our canceled honeymoon on 10 months later. The same ship that randomly at 3 am I went out to our balcony and sobbed, deep cathartic cries of missing my mom. I talked out loud to her into the blackness of night over the ocean about my life. I talked about missing her but being happy otherwise. I told her all the random things I would have if she were alive. Then I remembered that right before the call with the medium, I asked my mom to bring up that conversation on the ship as a sign. Wow. She sure did, I almost missed that sign.

Months later I noticed a song on the radio all the time. Once I remember walking into the garage and that song was on, I got goose bumps from it. I'd heard it in the car often as well. Each time I would have a physical reaction of knowing to it, yet I never took time to listen to the words. One night I was reading a book by Allison DuBois (the show *Medium* is based on her) and she talked about her dad that had passed on and how he would communicate with her through song. I loved imagining that possibility. That next morning, I went to a business meeting and on my way home I turned on the radio and that same song that I kept hearing was just beginning. This time, for the first time, I listened to the words. I was stunned. Here are some of the lyrics,

"Yes, I understand that every life must end, aw-huh,..
As we sit alone, I know someday we must go, aw-huh,..
Oh, I'm a lucky man, to count on both hands the ones I love,"
The last line of the song is, *"meet you on the other side"*.

I sat and cried, somehow caught perfectly between disbelief and certainty. When I got home and looked it up online. I studied the words and listened to it over and over, it was so healing. Then I paid attention to whom it was by... Pearl Jam... yep, another pearl reference. Mom, you are amazing! The song was released the year she died, yet I was not aware of it until all the above happened in 2011.

I have never looked for anyone to agree with me or validate these signs, I do not care. We all have our comfort levels based on what we are scared to know because of fear and our experiences. We can be afraid of the unknown and also fear that religion has pushed on us. (I highly recommend the book "Messages from Spirit" by Colette Baron-Reid where she gets into when the Church transitioned from working with spirit mediums to instilling fear about them because they conflicted with the church's agenda... fascinating read). For me I have found peace as a Christian, but I also believe in an afterlife, the beauty that can come from communicating, trusting, learning, and working with Angels. I also have found peace in parts of messages from other religions and spiritual teachings as well. Instead of getting caught up in the religious rules and fear that can sometimes be taught, I try to live like Jesus did. I use him as the goal, not the church.

When we have lost someone we love, our biggest shift can come when we stop focusing so much on their passing and instead start to focus on the gratitude for their time in our lives. Reframe from only remembering their death, to our experiences shared, lessons taught and learned, and the love we gave and received. When we can pull ourselves from the anger of not having longer and instead sit in gratitude for having what we did have it can unlock us from the loop of deep grief we are replaying in our minds. I finally started realizing that my mom lived a whole life of love and making a difference in her 57 years. She was done, called home. I do not have to agree with it, or even fully understand it. It does give me a way to reframe her death into imagining her seeing her dad again, past friends, and brings me peace to imagine that there is a larger divine game plan she is a part of. Honoring those 57 years also helps honor her life, why she was here, the differences she made. Once we can balance out the grief with appreciation, a new level of healing occurs.

Be Gentle with Yourself

A few years ago, I sat cross-legged on the living room floor of our small house. I had the bottom doors swung wide open of the entertainment center and I had pulled out every photo album I could find. I had a goal. While I gathered the photos, I was reviewing in my mind what a failure I was when it came to my body; I had put on 20 lbs. during 2009 in the months following my mom's death and during an ectopic pregnancy. Follow that up with having Aspen in 2010 and the baby weight that came from it.

I decided enough was enough. I gathered up all the photos I could find of myself to use as proof to leverage myself into taking back control of my body. My goal was clear; I would get so angry and ashamed of my body that I would propel myself full into a body change.

I continued looking through photos from 2008 and my wedding that year. Then 2009 from the first day of our honeymoon, to later in February as I stood holding my new nephew. I made a mental note of how that burgundy tank top in the photo used to look cute and now was tight and I had to wear a sweater over it to disguise the added weight in my stomach area. (Thank you iced coffee and cheese trays). I looked at photos of me from 2010 holding my new baby. I piled up every photo that had a double chin, a stomach role, even a bad angle. This was about to go down on record as the quickest shaming session ever.

What happened next is truly amazing, a gift of grace. Instead of feeling shame, the more I looked through those photos the more I looked at this woman who was holding it all together. I recognized myself as a woman who survived the toughest years of her life. I survived multiple moves across the country during my twenties, a divorce, essentially being a single mom for a few years until meeting the love of my life and getting remarried.

I saw a body that held me as I stood next to the casket that held my dear mom. I saw a body that provided comfort to a young daughter daily and eyes that lit up when she would see her husband. A strong woman who despite those hard times was genuinely creating a happy life.

I sobbed as I grieved for this girl who missed her mom, who was raising a baby and all that comes with that. I sobbed for this woman who was running a business and making that work. Surprisingly, I no longer felt any shame in those pictures that day. Instead I found myself rooting for that girl. That girl did not need a critic, she needed support. I finished those few hours of reflection and basked in the healing powers of it. I am still here. That year of grief did not destroy me, my story gets to continue.

I knew I needed to love my body, but better health was no longer going to happen by beating myself up emotionally. It was going to be from honoring myself and loving myself. That created a huge shift in perspective.

Compassion. I am pretty good as showing others compassion but have not always been the best at doing so for myself. We all deserve better than this, imagine what can happen when we focus on the good. We can celebrate our strengths and show ourselves a grace during hard times.

Loss is hard. We all respond differently. Some will either gain weight or forget to eat, others will drink too much, and others might start spending. They are all rooted in the same place. Feel the feelings. Trust that you can handle the feelings. Trust that you will grow from this experience, this experience will help you help others. Honor yourself and know that you can feel all the feelings and not be defined the feelings. Try to shift your perspective to seeing how strong you are. Even in sadness, in mourning, in rebuilding... see your strength. Point it out to yourself when notice growth in your spirit and in your healing. Honor the process, be gentle with yourself.

The First Big Holidays After

The love of one person can light up a holiday and leave the memories forever perfect in our minds.

 Here is a passage I wrote in 2014. *Thanksgiving is next week. We have no plans. My grandma is in her 90's now and had to quit hosting dinner for the holiday a couple years ago. Going to her house was our family tradition my whole life until then. We would pack into the car and drive two hours north. Up, up, and then over the big hill to see Lake Superior spread out in front of us, we were almost there. Delicious food, cousins, aunts, and uncles would all pack together in her house for a few hours. Most of the men watched sports downstairs, while us women were catching up and playing with the kids upstairs. There were always homemade pies and I can still picture the scalloped potatoes served up on china. In my mind are clear visions of mini turkey shaped salt and pepper shakers, bowls of candy corn and after dinner mints in the middle of the tables. After dinner we would look through the upcoming sale ads together and plan gift exchanges. It was magical.*

 Together all of us cousins would make lists of what gifts we wanted as kids, circling photos in the sale ads. Years later we would plan out what we might get our own kids. A few times I was lucky enough to experience holidays with my daughter, my mother, and her mother.

 This year my in-laws are all out of town, each traveling. I have not heard if there is a celebration on my dad's side. I hope so. I now realize how much my mom helped pull together these holiday gatherings, even on my dad's side.

 For the first 30 years of my life I took these events for granted, the smell of my mom's perfume and the heat of the rollers all on their metal pegs. We would watch until the red dots on top of each roller turned brown, then we knew the rollers were hot enough. I would watch my mom set her hair, get all 5 of us kids together and my father would drive us all. Talk radio about fixing cars would fill the long ride.

 There is a hole right now though as I think back. I am in an in-between space. Not able to go back in time, yet not having new traditions to look ahead to. This will be my 6th Christmas without my mom's glowing festivities and tangible happiness. It is amazing how much one person can do to make a holiday perfect for so many others. As an adult now, I do not know how she did it.

The house always had a warm glow. The Christmas tree was decorated with dozens of handmade ornaments from all throughout the years. Sometimes another smaller tree would be decorated with more formal, matching ornaments in the front window. I can still hear the Christmas music playing throughout the house. I distinctly remember the smell of pine, cookies, candles, and food. More than that, there was a loving energy. Anyone was welcome. There was anticipation and magic in the air. Having everyone together was another opportunity for my mom to try out new recipes. One year she spoiled us with steak or lobster, another we tested spinach and ricotta stuffed pasta shells. There were always meatballs, cheeses, and homemade rice pudding.

Looking back at my writing while here now in the present; it is heartbreaking how holidays change so much after someone we have spent so many with is no longer here. That first Christmas I was caught between wanting to head the Caribbean to pretend Christmas was not happening and recreating the perfect Christmas in my mom's honor. It all felt so heavy, the holidays were arriving whether I was ready emotionally or not.

It has now been a decade and there have been happy celebrations and those with a feeling of emptiness with my siblings and their families. What keeps me moving forward is that I want my kids to have memories like I did. I am much simpler in my approach to holidays, but the amount of love is the same.

Sometimes I have fallen back on doing the minimum. I play Christmas music; pull out a favorite tablecloth and serve dinner on beautiful dishes. It all works to create a feeling of home and comfort. It even helps bring a little of the magic to my tender heart. I have started to really notice and appreciate those who make the effort to bring magic to the holidays. I have since talked to people who have kept their past traditions and others who changed things up completely. I do not think there is any perfect answer that lessens the pain for us. When we look outside our grief, there may be people who value their holidays with us, and others hoping to find someone to share those times with.

I focus less now on gifts, and more on those I get to be with. I savor gatherings with family and friends. As time has passed, I have learned that not every family has someone like my mom was. She was a gatherer of people, a light, someone who made the holidays come alive. I do realize though that we can become that for others. Ione, my mother in law embodies this spirit as well. In my husband's family they often get together after Christmas and we all meet at a hotel, lodge, rented cabin, or something similar and spend the weekend together. Ione always arrives a little early with totes of decorations to transform the rented space into a beautiful Christmas feel. Tablecloths, floral arrangements, and themed centerpieces come together into a meaningful showing of her love for us. I try to learn what I can from my mom's memory and from Ione; we can all honor our loved ones who have passed on and those with us by embodying and emulating what we loved most about our holidays together with them.

Here are some ideas to bring your loved one into your holiday; make a meal they loved or their favorite drink, play music they enjoyed, hang a remembrance ornament on the tree to honor them, talk about your loved one, go around the room and share your favorite memories or funny stories. Our first Christmas after my mom passed, all the girls in our family each wore one of my mom's cheesy, "ugly" Christmas sweaters. It was a subtle way to feel her around while also lightening the mood a bit.

My wish for everyone missing someone this time of year is to know you are not alone, may you find small spots and pockets of joy. Feeling those moments of joy does not mean you have forgotten your deceased loved one, re-frame it that they would not want their legacy to be sad holidays. For this first Christmas, Thanksgiving, birthday, or other holiday the goal may be to simply get through it in one piece. Take the pressure off, especially if your loss was recent. Honor your needs as well. Schedule some stress-free down time, bring extra mascara.

Remembering her for:

The fearless 10 year old girl she was on rollerskates

bravely barreling own the sidewalk

waving at everyone she passed as she
took in the sights, sounds and smells.

She knew she was going to make a difference
in this world and she she sure did.

So she allowed herself to just be where she was
and let her mind open up to all that was around her.

— Noelle

Say Her Name

Mom. Nancy. Wife. Daughter. Sister. Aunt. Friend. No matter what she was called, she is one of my favorite people, and I was incredibly lucky to have her as my mom. Please say her name; please continue to talk about her with me. As I have strived to keep my mom's name and memory alive in my life, in conversations and life situations I have started to put people in groups based on our interactions. I believe each group is full of good intentions, our approaches and comfort zones for discussing the deceased are varying.

The sharers

The "sharers", these are people, who are like me, and love to talk about those who have passed. It feels good to share how much my mom loved certain events. When one of her grandkids does something funny, I laugh as I imagine what her response would have been if she were still alive. I wonder what she would have thought about some tough life choices we've each had to make since she has passed. The sharers are the people who easily and often lightheartedly let conversations drift between those who have died and life now. Oftentimes, they are also the people who have experienced loss themselves. They know it feels good to have their loved acknowledged, remembered, and honored.

The supportive

The supportive friends and family; this group will have a conversation with you about someone who has passed but will not initiate said conversation. For this group, conversation initiation is out of their comfort zone. I love these people for trying though. They want to be supportive but may be unsure if bringing up a deceased love one will cause pain. This group may also start to give off a guarded feeling when the conversation begins about the deceased. I believe this is unintentionally and often a result of them striving to be empathetic. It would be easy to assume this group has not had a lot of experience with death themselves, but that is not necessarily true.

There are times I can tell a friend catches herself bringing up her own mother and stops for a second as if to evaluate whether it is appropriate. Let me be clear. Talk to me about your mom, it brings me so much joy that we can share a conversation about her. If I cry during the conversation, those tears should not be scary. I will feed off your intentions more than if you say the "wrong" thing. If your intentions are good, I focus on that. Your heart and support are appreciated.

The "shut the conversation down'ers"

The third group I call the "shut the conversation down" group. To this group I plead, "Please say her name." I would explain to them, the tender, sacredness in the days following my mom's death. I spent countless hours shuffling through every memory I could. Even while I recounted the days and weeks leading up to her death, contemplating if there was something I could have done, I was getting to spend time with her and her memory. I was reliving experiences, with her, in my mind; trying to anchor every moment and memory in my brain. Even through tears, these memories are such a gift. It means I get to experience her so strongly that it feels real. Think about that; after someone is gone and we do not know if we'll ever feel close to him or her again, a memory can pop up that is so fresh, so real they pull us close for a moment. For that moment, our lives are intertwined.

Please do not be afraid to share memories with me. If you find an old photo that includes her; please share. If you are angry with her for leaving us too soon, that is okay. It is all okay. There is no perfect thing you must say. Just be there, allow me to talk, allow me to feel. If you have someone you know who has lost a parent, a baby, a grandparent, a friend; give them the chance to heal, to talk about their loved one. Allow them to bounce between laughing at a fun memory and crying because they are gone.

The helpers

This group of people can fall into any of the first three groups. I admire the people that came forward in the days after my sweet mom passed, including our family friend Marilyn who brought over food and the other neighbors and friends who checked in. Even now, years later I wish I were more like these people. The loved ones who walked into that situation and were not put off by the heaviness or the ever-ranging span of emotions we were all feeling. They kindly offered non-judging support and space for us to just be. They would slip in and out, checking in on us. My husband and I had only been married 7 months when my mom passed. I am forever grateful to him. He did the dishes every night for weeks; taking care of every detail of our lives while I spent time with my dad and siblings. These helpers are the same people who also tend to set up the meal calendars; they show up with a note or gift, even when they are not sure what to say. I have seen calendars for people to come and clean a house, bring meals, or gift cards, rides for kid's schedules. What a gift those people are who step up and carry the heartbroken through the toughest moments. We need to make sure to appreciate and thank the helpers. We also need to find ways to give back to the helpers. Some will give and give until one day they wake up and resent us for taking advantage of their generosity. They will often appear as if they have everything together in their own lives, so keep an eye on ways they could use a hand. Most of them would never think of asking. Protect them and return the help. God bless the helpers.

Not shockingly, we each handle grief differently, regardless of which of the three groups we fit into. Some people pull select people in close as their safe group. It is their way of holding on and getting through. To those on the outside of that circle, I say, "do not take it personal, just be there when they are ready." Check in when you can and hold a space for them to build their inner strength until they are able to talk about it.

Other people may be better at pretending everything is normal and as it always was. People force themselves through each day afraid to be swallowed whole by the memories and grief. With the pressure of certain days like weddings, holidays, birthdays the hole does feel larger.

The tears are less now but do not be afraid if they show up. Tears do not mean I am upset she came up; it means I love her. To talk about and miss her is my way to continue to pull her into the now, to acknowledge and honor that she was here. Do not let my tears make you nervous. You do not need to help me stop crying. Also, do not think I do not miss her if I am joyful in my life. It is all okay. Thank you for having the courage to say her name. Thank you for allowing me space to continue to let her be a part of my now.

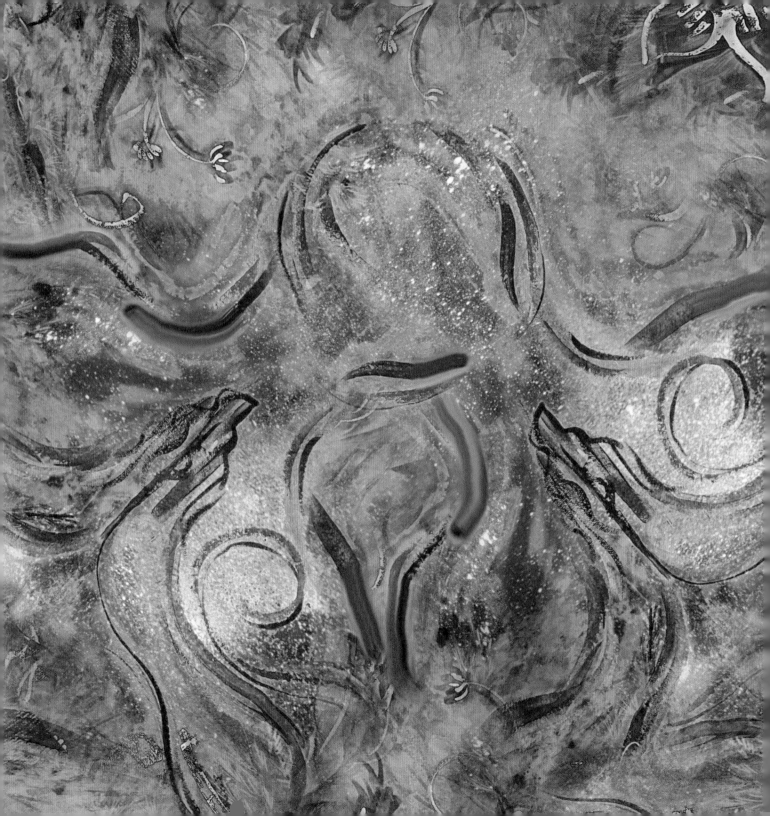

Sharing the Same Dream

My mom has now been gone for almost 4 years. Today is her birthday so I decided to share my story of an experience that my husband and I had shortly after she passed. I was getting ready to climb into bed and my husband was already asleep. I felt a strange feeling and was drawn to the wall on the side of my bed. I didn't see anything but definitely felt a presence. I woke up the next morning and my husband was already sitting at the kitchen table.

I had had a very vivid dream about my mom and I was about to tell my husband about it when suddenly he said, "I had the strangest dream about your mom." I said that I did too and told him to tell me about it. He said that he didn't really feel like it was a dream but more of a "visit." He said that he dreamt that he looked over at me while we were lying in bed and saw me staring at the wall on the side of my bed. He looked at the wall and could see the image of my mom's face projected on the wall along with other images of my mom when our children were little.

I about fainted when my husband described his dream because that is exactly what happened in my dream. I saw my mom projected on the wall; I saw other images of my mom with our kids. Everything my husband described. We wondered how we could possibly dream the same dream but soon realized that my mom was just popping in to let us both know that she's still here with us.

Christie Cassady

When We Can't Save Someone

We were scheduled to be on our honeymoon, so no one was expecting to hear from us. This made the first week after my mom's passing much easier, logistically. We were not expected at work, Skylar was not expected at school. There were no sports, no appointments, no bills to be paid. We were left to focus one hundred percent on each other, my mom's funeral, and our family. It was a gift.

The second week Skylar went back to school, and Bruce returned to work. I spent many of my days back in my hometown at my parents' house. I lived off leftovers from the funeral luncheon. It was more cheese, bread, and crackers than any person should ever have; but it was easy and delicious.

I was still getting supportive online messages and cards from people who were only now hearing the news. I was so grateful for my family; we could bounce between laughing and crying without judgment. We could also vent a bit about some of my mom's life choices without having it dilute the love we also felt. This was a safe place for us to share our truest feelings. Our sad, complicated feelings.

My mom, Nancy died of undetected pancreatitis. In the emergency room on a Friday afternoon, the doctor chose not to run tests, check her blood, or urine. They misdiagnosed her as having back spasms and sent her home with painkillers. After getting home she laid in bed, my dad made a sandwich, sat next to her, and watched something on TV. She fell asleep. A little while later he looked over at her and she was not breathing. This story breaks my heart in so many ways. First, for my dear dad who loved this woman and could not save her. Next for my younger brother who tried CPR on her until the paramedics arrived. For a long time, I had wished I could go back in time and have the doctors take her blood, or urine, or run tests that would have revealed that she was hours from death. I wished that I could rewind to months before and have my mom disclose to her long-time doctor that she was secretly drinking in excess. Maybe the doctor would have chosen different medications to give her or done something different.

My mom was like so many other women. She put everything she had into raising five kids, working, and creating a nice home for us all. Then in her forties as my dad's business grew, she was able to quit her nursing job and be home more for us kids. This was wonderful for our family for many years. She was able to be at all our sporting and school events as well as get to know us and our friends better. We all got to see her more, she was a rock we each had by our sides.

As us kids got older, and moved out one by one, she lost certainty about where she fit into the world. She had so much talent and heart and did not know where to use it. I can only guess her pride was involved a bit too, as starting over in a career seemed too extreme. My parents lived in an upper, middle-class neighborhood, drove nice cars, and seemed to have it all figured out. From what I can piece together, she was lonely, and she could not see her way forward clearly. A few years before her passing she had a knee replacement, menopause set hold, and there were some painful times for her kids (including my divorce) that she could not make better for us. I think it was the perfect storm of physical and emotional changes and she was swallowed whole by it.

When I first moved back from Texas, and was going through my divorce, my mom and I would have fun wine and cheese nights. We would watch old movies together; or make wreaths, topiaries, or some other craft project. My sisters would often be there too. This time together was a gift.

What we were not aware of at the time, was that this occasional wine drinking was getting more frequent when we were not around. My mom started (what I would call) self-medicating for pain and insomnia with alcohol after her surgery. She was prescribed sleeping pills and something for anxiety. Those pills mixed with alcohol were not good. It is worth emphasizing that this was a woman who only had a single drink or two a year my entire life until the last few years of her life. She was not a typical drinker. Even during this time, it was not obvious. She did not go to bars, she did not drink at restaurants, and she did not drink at dinner. How could she be facing this now in her fifties? As signs of her drinking revealed themselves a couple of years later, we were not able to reconcile it all. It was not the "her" we knew. It did not make sense. We were all too close to see it all with a proper perspective. Our love clouded it all up.

Eventually, when things did start to reveal themselves, a year or two before my mom passed, my sister and I staged an intervention with her. After hours of exhaustive, barren research trying to find the right facility that our family could both afford and would fit her needs (somewhere between depression and alcohol dependency) we were frustrated and starting to feel hopeless. Finally, a call to a hospital and a hopeful discussion. They assured us that if we could get our mom to their Emergency Room when she was intoxicated, they could hold her and transfer her into the correct facility.

What happened next was heart breaking. It took us days to convince our dad to let us do this. He was sure things would work themselves out. My dad is great at many things but when it comes to decisions, he would rather put the decision off. His goal from my perspective is typically to delay the decision until he can come up with enough data to make the perfect decision. This case was no different. However, not deciding.... was indeed making a decision. He eventually agreed to not stand in our way. After approaching our mom and begging her to go get help, she reluctantly agreed. My dad was heartbroken seeing his wife feel ambushed. Although at this point, he did support our efforts... As we were getting ready to leave the house and head to the hospital my mom said she needed to change clothes; we gave her a few minutes of privacy in her bathroom. Concealed from us, she was literally "chugging" vodka in there. Saying goodbye to it in an ironic sense. By the time we got to the hospital thirty miles away, she was flat out drunk. She stumbled as she walked from the car to the hospital entrance. The details after this are fuzzy to me; mostly because my mom made sure from that point on to keep us completely in the dark. What I know is that they transferred her to a different facility, and she refused all contact with us. It was days later when my dad was able to pick her up. She did an excellent job convincing him that he was the only one that understood her. Her anger at all of us was unlike it had ever been in our lives. My mom refused to talk about where she had been; she only referred to it as "the hole". Within weeks she had convinced my dad that she could handle a fun drink here and there. They formed an alliance and essentially told the rest of us, they were "handling it" from now on.

My dad's most frustrating fault to me, during all of this was being blinded by love. Years later, I realized this could also be called an "enabler". He wanted to believe his wife of over 30 years. He wanted to love her back to health. My sister and I were left frustrated and upset. We had tried to help and failed. Had we misjudged? Were we over-reacting? Both the hospital and the treatment center felt like no help. There was no follow-through, no way to force her to stay plugged into a program. I remember having numerous crying sessions with my sister and us having to surrender our wishes and decide to simply love our mom. We would agree to disagree; we would stop the fight and let her be. We also acknowledged out loud that we had to accept that this might kill her. It seemed far-fetched and abstract, but it was said. Her drinking did improve after that, or maybe she hid it better. The subject was pushed into the background moving forward. After this, she did not drink in front of us.

A couple of weeks before my mom died, I had a long conversation with her. She was crying about feeling sad and wanting to feel like her old self again. She could not shake the layers of shame and emotions that clung to her. She longed for the simpler times of her life. She questioned if she had been a good enough mom. I was able to tell her how amazing our lives were because of her. I thanked her for all she's done and listed example after example of the ways she was a great mom and grandma.

Next, we talked about working together to makeover her bedroom and bathroom. It would be a fun project and (not knowing the continued depths of her drinking, medications, and illness at the time) it seemed like a good way for her to re-find herself and her joy again. For her birthday I gave her a few decorating and remodeling magazines for inspiration. When I gave them to her, she did not remember us having a conversation about the bathroom. I found myself re-explaining it to her. Looking back there were a few times like this. The time we went to see a movie in a theatre, then the following week we saw a commercial for that same movie and she said that it looked good. She had no recollection of already seeing it. At the time I attributed these things to her medications, ever since she had been taking them it was as if chunks of time would be missing for her. It was scary. It would be a few years later that we would see more in the news about one of these prescription drugs and the horror stories about it; long after she had passed.

I am telling my mother's story in a way that is truthful from my perspective, but it comes with truckloads of guilt. She is not here to tell her side. I would never, ever want someone to think less of her because of anything I have shared. I have including it in this book because I know there are so many women like her. Women who are giving, loving, and strong who have had times of struggle behind the scenes. Their shame only adds to their struggle. For some it is drinking, other's it is prescription meds, gambling, shopping, depression, eating disorders, or something else. I wish we talked more openly about this time of life for women.

In trying to help my mom there was a very heavy, unspoken expectation; *we do not air family business*, we do not need to discuss the embarrassing or hard stuff. When I went through my divorce year ago and talked so openly about it, I sensed the perplexed, and sometimes disapproving responses of my older relatives. Their guarded energy did not come as a surprise when it came to my mom.

We found a lack of accessible, mental health care for women just like her. Women who want to keep their dignity and are not sure what type of

81

help they need... They just know they feel sad, lonely; a bit depressed, and because of that they are self-medicating in some form. It felt like a betrayal to say she needed rehab. She needed to fix the sadness, so she did not feel the need to self-medicate. Ironically, she also needed to get sober to truly fix the sadness. As a society, women need our extra love and support during the second half of life. These are the times when children move out and begin their own lives, careers change courses, parents age and need help; each of these alone can be life altering. When you mix them with possible health issues and the decades when women are in menopause while hormones are changing as well; it can leave women feeling just like my mom did. We need to find ways to support these women, ways to help them re-connect their gifts with the world, all without shame.

Looking back, I believe my mom knew on a soul level, that her time was near. She never said this or probably even thought about it consciously but there were astonishing things that happened in the weeks leading up to her death that lead me to this conclusion. My mom died on January 30th. A few weeks prior, in December, my parents got a video camera. My family has only a handful of videos from the previous 30 years of our life or events. Those last 7 weeks however, there were 28 videos recorded. There were videos of my mom at each of the relatives' Christmas celebrations along with random day-to-day moments, and her last birthday party too. This was such a gift. In addition to the videos, the week before my mom died, she got back in touch with an old high school friend. They had not spoken in decades. That week they caught up. Then two days before she passed, my parents had gone to my Grandparents' house. My dad's parents lived just a few miles from us for 20 years, so we had been to their home thousands of times. This time however, for the first time, my mom walked up and down the hallway looking at every photo of the relatives, asking about each one. In doing this she unknowingly gifted my Grandparents with conversations about loved ones that they would cherish for years to come. The day before she died, my mom had a long talk with her mom. During this talk she let her mom know that after decades of hurt, she had finally forgiven her dad. Even though her dad had passed back in 1994, my mom had held onto her hurts and frustrations about their relationship for her whole life, until the eve of her passing. Piece by piece, person by person, various loose ends were tied, bringing bits of peace to those around my mom during her passing.

I have spent so many hours and days thinking back to what I wish we could have done differently. I wish we would have risked embarrassing my mom to save her. Yet I wonder, would continuing to push for her to quit drinking or changing her prescriptions have helped? Could we have left a message with her doctor or would it have created a divide during her last years? I wish I had magical words of inspiration that would have helped her see her gifts and the steps to take to embrace them. Instead, we are left with unknowns and empathy. My heart breaks for my mom. This amazing woman was swallowed whole by life; her love of others, and the inability to help us all in our own heartaches.

I have chosen to learn every lesson I can from her. There were countless lessons she taught me herself while she was alive. There were so many I have learned through her death and final years as well. Including, taking on everyone else's drama, and trying to carry their pain for them; it can kill you. I have a natural tendency towards guilt and shame around things I have little control over, did I learn this behavior? Some examples of areas where shame or guilt arises in me: not being bolder, not being fun enough, and even something as simple as putting a baseball cap that feels too small can send me into a shame spiral about how my weight has made my head too big. One time when I was in junior high, I walked into the bathroom in our home and saw a large unrolled pile of gauze. It was covered in dried blood. My reaction was not to ask the family about it, *what if I embarrassed someone or created an uncomfortable conversation for someone*? So instead of asking, I carefully gathered up the gauze and put it on the top shelf of the bathroom closet. It was days later that I learned it had been created to be part of my brother's upcoming Halloween costume. I had to laugh, but also examine what made me want to hide it for someone? Was it a healthy empathy, or something deeper and unhealthy? Did my mom carry this pattern in her life as well? What could I do to overcome this? What can I do going forward to not carry others' problems yet still care? These questions have shaped much of my learning over the last decade.

It can feel so lonely in this world while grieving. Life continues moving forward around us as we work to accept our new reality. The first time I felt alone in an abyss of "left behind-ness" was when my oldest was just a toddler and I was in my mid-twenties. My friends were starting careers, buying nice cars, even homes. *How would I ever catch up?* I wondered. I can only imagine how left behind and lonely my mom felt after raising five kids and looking up and feeling like society was flying by her... without her. Whether from grief or life, loneliness and feeling left behind can be devastating.

There are so many of us each feeling alone in our stories and in our grief. We often feel shame because we know we are smart and strong, yet we cannot always navigate this time, especially alone. Reach out. There are online grief groups, groups offering hope, in person meetings and clubs, therapists, psychologists, and psychiatrists, pastors. Whether for help with grief, or you are feeling like my mom did; reach out. Your story does not end here. Use the hard times for the greater good. If you must go through this time of mourning or difficulty, is there some greater lesson or gift you can also harvest from it? The lessons from our grief and personal trials can help others, give us perspective, and even honor our loved ones that we have lost.

Visitors from Heaven During Final Days of Life

My Grandpa Franklin was a medic during WWII, a sports fanatic, a junior high counselor, a teacher, a storyteller, and a jokester. During 2019, I spent time with my Grandpa while recording his stories from WWII and life in general. One story he shared really stuck with me. It is about the time his medical evacuation unit cared for prisoners just released from the Bergen-Belsen concentration camp in Germany. My Grandpa shared about how one of the men rescued was so thin from starvation they could not give him the medical shots he needed because there was nothing between his skin and bones to put the needle into. He shared how they would feed this man a spoonful of broth every hour and start to build him back up over days. His eyes were staring off past me as he told this story, I could feel him re-living it as he shared. He talked of wonderful civilians they met and were able to help during the war. As I listened, I tried to imagine the weight of all he'd seen as a young man. He often wondered if he had done enough in this life, if he'd made enough of a difference. This was the theme of our visits often.

My Grandpa Franklin standing with the painting I did of him playing the harmonica in 2009:

In the spring of 2020 Grandpa Franklin had a heart attack, I headed to the ER after hearing the news, When I arrived, he was in good spirits. He was 94 and his doctors did not believe he would survive the surgery it would require to repair his heart. So instead the doctors and nurses focused on keeping him comfortable. We did not know if we had one hour with him or one day, any time beyond that would be a gift. Family from around the country flew in, we gathered around, we shared with him our gratitude and thanked him for being in our lives.

He told jokes to his Great Grandchildren who had come to visit. Those of us who could, came back again and sat with him the next day. He slept a lot but also had times where he spoke long stretches of Finnish and made a special point to have a moment of connection with each person there.

We watched as he slept, Sure that his time was near, his breathing was starting to get a rattle sound to it. Several times the nurse on duty forewarned us that he might pass within hours. I learned to value this helpful guidance and also ignore it. We watched as a cousin came from out of state and introduced him to his newest Great Grandchild. He had a special reaction to her and even wanted to hold her. There were countless beautiful moments like this each day.

When Grandpa Franklin seemed confused or somewhat awake and I was there, I would explain to him that his body was tired, he was in the hospital, he had a heart attack. I told him that his body is having a hard time, it was tired after 94 years and the time was getting near for him to go to Heaven. Each of us took turns over those days sharing our favorite stories that included him and assuring him it was okay to go, telling him we would watch over each other and our Grandma. At one point my Grandpa announced that he could see his brother. "He's driving a grader, he's so happy." A grader is what we, at least in the Midwest, call the tractor that goes down the dirt roads and combs them, evening them back out from bumps and potholes. A few minutes later his mom appeared to him sitting in a rocking chair. A few minutes more and he saw his dad. He talked about what they were each doing as he looked beyond us. I will never forget my aunt Janet being so affirming and making sure he knew how special that was. We all celebrated the gift of loved ones surrounding him. What a beautiful, comforting thought to imagine those who have died before us being there to welcome us. It also eases the sadness I have for myself a bit, knowing he will be joining loved ones that he loves dearly and misses.

On the fourth night, my sister and I stayed the night with him, we were grateful to relieve my aunt and Grandma on the overnight shift and let them get some sleep. Angie and I were each on a side of my grandpa. As he shifted in bed a bit and started to open his eyes for the first time in hours, we told him, "We are here Grandpa. It's Angie and Noelle. We are taking good care of you. We're here, we love you."

Unexpectedly, my grandpa opened his mouth, "Love you," he quietly said. Then miraculously he lifted his arms and gave us both a hug at the same time. He smiled as he held on to us. Hours later he was smiling, and we could tell he was somewhat awake again. He stared off beyond us, "it's very beautiful." he said. We openly talked to my Grandpa about Heaven and dying and the process. We asked our Grandpa to say hello to our mom when he sees her, to give her a big hug. We also asked him to send us a sign or visit us in our dreams. He looked at us slightly perplexed and humored but agreed. It felt strange asking but also, we knew it was our only chance to have the direct conversation with him.

Night five around two am my Grandpa started waking a bit again. These overnight moments of clarity he had were a true gift and becoming rarer. I asked my Grandpa what he was seeing or thinking about. He replied, "I'm not sure if I'm ready. I'm trying to find someone to follow through." We were not 100% sure what he meant but encouraged him that it was okay to follow that person through to the other side. I must note: my Grandpa also was a basketball player and coach for many years, one that was particularly obsessed with learning the fundamentals. So, I recognize the slight chance that he was using basketball terminology that night while talking about follow through.

Later that night, my Grandpa started to speak again, "I'm thinking about what it's like to be dying." I asked him what it's like. He said, "I'm not sure yet." These overnight visits were sacred to me for these treasured moments of insight into what he was experiencing and for the time to catch up with my uncles who would stay late or come early to help.

My Grandparents were approaching their 70th wedding anniversary the coming summer, my grandma talked to my Grandpa about what a great life they had together. I am grateful that we hired a documentary photographer to come and take photos during their 65th anniversary party four years prior. Pam Dusbabek at Heart of life photography captured so many beautiful images of my grandparents and them with. If you ever have a chance to hire a documentary photographer for a

family reunion, anniversaries, or special gathering, do it. On this page is one of the documentary photos.

After a week had passed and my grandpa was still hanging on, I re-learned the lesson I had with Ralphie. None of us know when the time is. We said our goodbyes. We all gave him permission to go and encouraged him to see his parents and grandparents. It was not yet his time, he continued to stay with us day after day. Relatives from out of town came and went as they could.

We had a rotation of over a dozen people helping and I still found it difficult to balance kids, work, household needs, and plan the perfect times to be with my grandpa. We observers have no control in the situation, there is no easy to way be a caretaker. As each day passed and I said goodbye and came home to do laundry, get some work done, help with homeschooling, and sleep I surrendered that I may not be the one to hold his hand when his time came. I had to surrender that this was between him and God. I had to get my ego out of it; my desire to be with him when he passed had to be put aside.

After losing my own mom unexpectedly and not getting to say goodbye, I really cherished this gift of being able to talk to my Grandpa over those first few days. I looked around at his 6 kids that had gathered and knew their world would never be the same after this week. I also knew it was a gift that they were able to say goodbye, care for him, and hear from him that he loved them.

As a society we tend to honor births exclusively but there is a beautiful sacredness to being able to sit with someone facing death as well. Another type of transition, an honoring of their life. In my Grandpa's case, there was gratitude of a long-lived life and a surrendering that it was his time. This felt very different to me in comparison to losing my mom unexpectedly and in her fifties.

Wednesday morning, I had my son Aspen get up at 4:30am with me. We got ready and headed to sit with my Grandpa once more. It was day nine since he had entered the hospital; he was no longer awake or talking. That morning I kissed my Grandpa's forehead and said hello, I sat on his right and later my Grandma joined me in holding his left hand. My dad arrived around 8 am and we sat together. After a while we decided to leave the room for a bit to give my Grandparents a little alone time.

After an hour or so we took our seats in his room again. Later that morning, tears rolled down my face as my Grandpa took his last breaths. I rubbed his chest and told him it was okay. We sat with him awhile after he passed and comforted my Grandma, who did not let go of his hand. She was his protector, his love. It was surreal and difficult, but his transition was full of love and support. I could only hope for any of us, when it is our time to go... may we be in our nineties and have our hands held by loved ones.

My Grandpa was a person I knew better than I knew most people in my life. He gifted us with stories from the war, growing up "up north", sports, travel, and stories from when him and my grandma were just starting out. My Grandpa had a Christmas Eve birthday, mine is Christmas day. There was a special bond between us, along with my sister who was born on New Year's Eve. We had over 50 years between us, but we shared many birthday parties together through the years.

"You've lived a good life. You have helped many people. You made such a difference." Those are the sentences we repeated to him most, not only during his final days but also during his final years. Those are the things that mattered in the end. A lesson we can all take with us. Live a good life. Help others. Make a difference where you can.

I am More Than This Partially Broken Me

It is amazing how life can change; 2008 - 2009 was such a pivotal time in my life. There was our wedding along the banks of the Mississippi, a first honeymoon attempt, a death, job change, a miscarriage, our dog Sam passed, a recession, a honeymoon re-do, a bankruptcy, an intervention, a dear friend with stage four cancer... it was a very full and emotional fourteen months.

I always believe that there are certain moments in our life where there is a figurative chapter change. Sometimes we invite these changes, other times we fight them. These are moments where we get to take our new reality and re-write the rules for our lives. We decide what we will focus on, we can reset our boundaries, re-decide what we are no longer going to accept, evaluate how we want to live our lives with a fresh clarity and a new outlook. Conveniently these are windows of time when others around us know things have changed and may not fight us as much while we make these changes. This may mean ending toxic relationships, finally going for a dream, or simply starting to use the good towels, dishes, and candles.

During these chapter changes, the part I like is retaking control. Normally when things feel so out of control in areas outside of my influence (hello pandemic), I can make lists and goals and take back enough of my power to feel stability. In the years following my mom's death however, there was something I was not prepared for. I did not know how to regain control of this situation; in fact, I hardly was able to define what I was experiencing while living it.

As I worked to put my life back together in the months and years following my mom's passing, I felt like many people were getting to know only the partially broken me. I had new husband, new in-laws, new neighbors, new parents of the teammates in my daughter's many sports, and a new family dynamic. I had the wind knocked out of me when my mom died. While I worked to re-find my footing, I had people criticize me with the most hurtful, deep judgments. I was used to feeling accomplished, strong, and appreciated. People in the past had always given me the benefit of the doubt, I was confident in how I fit into the world.

What people do not tell you about losing a best friend, a mom, at least for me was that I would deeply miss having that person who was always in my corner. She was always there to listen to any trouble I was having and give me perspective and reassurance. She was my person who would know my intention, she would tell when I was wrong. I could trust her. I am grateful my sisters were so supportive. (At least as much as they could be having 6 more babies between them in the decade since... they have had their own full plates.) My husband was a godsend as he listened to me work through my feelings over and over. Even with them though it took me a few years to heal enough to feel strong and speak up for my own needs without getting that validation from my mom.

I found out I was being berated behind the scenes by someone in my inner circle who had only ever appeared supportive to my face. This person attacked my career as an artist, my choice to work from home while raising the kids, he even told his own daughter not to turn out like me and be an artist. My whole life I had always been fully accepted as an artist. It was not something others looked down upon. I worked hard, studied my craft, made money, and I loved what I did, I had won the career lottery. I was not prepared for how deep it would hurt to have someone passive aggressively tear me apart. To attack the artist in me was to attack my way of life, my outlook, my heart, and my dreams. I was still so broken from grieving my mom that I could not properly put everything in correct perspective and appropriately handle this unexpected storm. It took me years to get to a place where this person's words did not matter. He was a coward who never said any of this to my face, instead it was shared to anyone else who would listen. I had to get real with myself and acknowledge that I would never want to live his life, I should not care if he did not understand mine. Normally though this is where having a mom who had my back would have outweighed this person's opinions. More than this person's words, I hated that they affected me. That frustrated me for years.

While still dealing with the above-mentioned person, one weekend I participated in a group art show. Not one person I knew came. Thankfully, there were others who shopped and visited but I felt so alone. I felt like a failure, so invisible and sorry for myself. In my mind I could see that obviously I suck at having friends and I have been delusional to think I have any artistic skill. The joke was on me, I could not even get people to show up to a local place to see me or my work, nobody cares. This hate spewing man was right, I should quit art.

I put a wall up after that experience. I did not want to feel vulnerable. I did not ever want to feel bombarded with someone else's doubt and judgment like I had in the years prior. I did not want any more sadness, it all hurt too much. This led me to multiple times of being ready to walk away from my art career. There were also countless times of feeling isolated, misunderstood, and angry. I was upset with everyone, mostly myself. I had tried to balance kids, work, life, marriage and had failed. Every six months or so I would end up hysterically crying during a breakdown. Why couldn't I get my career to the level I wanted? Why didn't others seem to care about me? Why did it feel like me against the world? This heartache led me down a very long but life changing path. My path to healing started one night while I was deep in the depths of uncertainty and despair. I wrote a private letter of anger laying out every part of my life and career that I was not okay with. Here is part of that letter:

I am tired of caring. I'm tired of caring more for others than they ever will for me. I realize I have been rewarding (in my own head) bonus points for being "nice". Points for including others, points for making others feel smart, strong, creative. I am a noticer. I thrive on noticing things. This includes life lessons. I often try to learn from other's mistakes so that I don't have to do the same stupid crap. So, thank you people, for being a teacher to me even though you didn't know you were.

My life has included multiple times of sticking up for the underdog and losing groups of friends at a time for doing so. I would always tell myself that I'd rather be the person who did what was right and that I was sure those same people would do the same for me. Have not seen most of those people since but points in my head for effort though, right?

Am I being unrealistic in what the world has to offer? Is this just how people treat one another, and I have just been blissfully ignorant to it? If I give up on the people around me who don't give back am I perpetuating that system that I try so hard to rise above? If I quit art for a while and instead spend time doing things for only me and my family will that help me re-establish my internal compass and make things clear again? Will it help replenish my heart?

I love the message and intention of my art so much that I'm terrified to let it take on a life of its own. I want so deeply for it to be out in the world that I'm gripping it too tight, I'm blocking it from the lives it's supposed to help. I am so "in it" that I cannot properly see it. I cannot tell where I end, and it begins.

The world needs people who are willing to see what is possible. It needs people to be dreamers when the world is full of people too scared to be vulnerable. I want to be one of those people. I want to make a difference. I want you to see me. Yet, I want to not need your opinion. I wish I could live in a bubble where I could create and give and never depend on anyone but that is not reality. I must sell my work, my ideas, my dreams to get to continue to play the game. I wish I did not feel let down so often.

I wish people would step up. Be real with me, be real with yourself. I wish we could truly see each other. I wish we were not all so busy so that we could be a friend to those who really matter to us. I wish as a society we could celebrate and honor people who live from their heart as much as we do those who talk most with their mouths.

Have I got it all wrong? Have I been kidding myself? I feel like there must be a mismatch in how I think I am versus how people perceive me. I am a strong person, does that translate to people that I don't need encouragement? That I will just figure it out? I play with that in my mind because yes, I am strong. I am smart, loving, and sensitive as well. However, as "strong" as I am, I am human. I do need support. I do need people in my corner.

I am partly embarrassed by that letter but mostly grateful I let it out. In writing that letter I had an epiphany. I had pushed people out. I realized I was not being vulnerable or fully honest with myself; I was not letting most people help or support me. I was only sharing my stories of success after I had knew how they would turn out. I was not letting others be with me on the journey to that success. I did not want to fail. I had to teach myself that it was okay to feel vulnerable and let others in again.

The second lesson I learned is that I was focusing on the wrong people and situations. There was indeed women in my life who knew and understood the real me. These were my people. They have been mentors to me in so many ways. They have been surrogate mothers to me, teachers, inspirations, and wise gifts of calm in a swaying decade, reminders to have fun. They validated me; the realest me. They also continued to accept me as I showed up.

Looking back, I can also see now with better perspective that I have loved spending time with my husband and being with my kids so much that I have devoted nearly all my time to them. Any other free time was spent with my dad and siblings. I have not been the best about reaching out to friends. Wow, maybe some of those things I wrote in my letter were true about me?

It is only now with years of perspective that I can see how my grief affected how I received that initial criticism about my career. In past times I am certain I could have brushed it off without a second thought. In this new reality though, nothing felt stable or secure. When that criticism intersected with grief it snowballed into years of doubt and anger at myself and the world.

I would have never guessed that grief would make me debate giving up a career I love. Yet, I can read it back to myself now with more clarity. I have always said that my art is a tool, it is my way of getting uplifting messages out into the world. I have recognized my own need to be seen and understood and I see the connection now to why I create art and gifts that can help others feel connected, understood, and seen.

In my letter I refer to being a noticer, I can look back with gratitude for this trait now instead of cursing it. My feeling heart has come full circle and I use these gifts now in my writing and my art unapologetically.

I share this story and my letter for anyone who has experienced loss. Grief is messy. Sometimes it does not feel like grief. It feels instead like anger, loneliness, frustration. It can be shown in the ways we ineffectively handle situations that under normal times would not have affected us. Gift yourself grace as you find your new footing.

I also share this for the sensitive hearts like me. Even without grief I clearly felt frustrations with the way I interacted with the world. I felt taken advantage of, empty, sad. I know I'm not alone in those feelings. Reaching that level of anger and resentment was a gift to me. In the years since I have learned to chill out tons more and give only when I will not be resentful if the giving is not reciprocated. I have had to recognize my role and thinking patterns, including how I fill my heart and needs. I also had to acknowledge where I was putting focus and too much need and where I was taking others for granted. This process would have helped me years before my grief journey, but I am grateful for it now.

I will never know how things would be if my mom was still here. So instead of sitting in an unsolvable pool of wishing she were still here and feeling sorry for myself, I am learning to break that pattern by reframing how I think of my years of grieving. I can instead focus on the layer of strength I have gained. I have also gained an understanding that being vulnerable, or grieving does not equal being weak. I have found a deeper appreciate for life and those around me and I am grateful for those things. My mom taught me so much about love, giving, helping, parenting, creating, marriage, and running a household. I am so grateful for those lessons. I see now that I was also able to learn valuable things from her even in her death. I was able to find a strength and depth of courage I had not known before. My mom would be so proud of me.

While time does help heal; mostly I do not mind this small hole in my heart, that is my mom's space. Even though my heart is full of amazing memories of my mom I do appreciate this little empty spot too, I do not really want to fully "heal" it. It is a connection to rawness, to the missing, to the unknown, to faith in the unseen, to my sweet mama.

The Grieving Superpower

I was talking with a friend as the one-year anniversary of her husband's passing was approaching, "Noelle, I feel like I'm in a freaking movie, like it can't be real. All the stuff happening." She went on to explain people who come into her life daily during the last year as if on cue to give her a message or sign. The perfectly "accidental" meeting of others with stories to share for her benefit. Odd meetings that she would have brushed off in the past, now she was hyper-focused on allowing them to unfold. I could not help but nod in agreement. Yes, I knew exactly what she was talking about. I call it the grieving superpower.

After losing someone who was a part of your daily life, there is a time that follows that event where life feels like our world has been busted into millions of pieces. Every daily routine now altered, every holiday forever changed, a buzzing of counter narrative rolls through our brains non-stop.

Imagine yourself in a tunnel, with laser like focus on processing one thing, grief. All attention is on trying to understand the loss, remembering your loved one, and figuring out how to move forward. All other sounds are now muffled in the background, things that seemed to matter before often seem frivolous during this time. This time, although a time I would not wish it on anyone… does bring its own gifts as well. It is a time before "real life" has sucked us back in.

Here are 7 ways to honor the superhero grief period:

1) Write in a journal – during this time of intensity it can feel as if things will be this clear and focused forever. Write things down. Write your feelings. Write your memories. Write all that you notice. Signs from spirit, dreams, the kindness of others, goals for your future. Write them all down. Continue writing when you feel anger, sadness, fear, and yes, even joys. During this time of hyper-awareness and simplified life it is the time to capture all that you can. You will be able to gift yourself with this written down account of everything later when you find yourself out of the tunnel.

2) Know that you are not alone – find your people. Sometimes those around us are understanding and can be an incredible support system. Other times we do not have people around that are able to be as supportive as needed. Find online grief groups, podcasts, read blogs, and books. You do not have to

experience this time alone. When we are so in tune with grief and our loss; it can leave everything else as a blur. Do not be afraid to find help to rejoin that outer world as well.

3) There is no proper timetable for grief – I have heard too many stories of a boyfriend or spouse, a boss, or well-meaning best friend expressing frustration that, "you're not over it yet?" In-laws who do not get it, friends or co-workers who seem annoyed that all you talk about is your loss, family who wants you to move forward and quit "moping". People try to understand but we all handle things differently. My advice is this: *trust your knowing*. Find people who can help you move forward and honor your grief. If you are not able to handle your career, your kids, your life then I encourage you to find help. Find a counselor, pastor, or therapist who can walk you through honoring your grief while also honoring your other life commitments. There are also online groups where you can share your feelings openly without fear judgment or fear of annoying those you love most. I share a few insights in the introduction chapter of this book as well about breaking the loops of circular grief patterns.

4) Gather wisdom – Is there something you could take from this unthinkable time that could help others? Is there a new perspective you have gained? Finding truth and wisdom does not mean you are glad the event happened. It means that if you have to walk through this fire… at least try to harvest what you can from it so you can reach out a hand to the next person to help them through the fire as well.

5) Find a way to honor the memory of your loved one. There are many options, find one that resonates with you or your loved one's personality. Write about them, create a photo album, find a creative outlet such as drawing or singing, crafting, cooking, or even redecorating. When my mom passed my sisters and I gathered up all her favorite recipes along with photos of her cooking with her grandchildren and put together a cookbook. That following Christmas we gave those cookbooks to all my mom's siblings and kept some for each of us. The process of creating that book allowed us hours of conversation and reliving memories of our mom in the process, it was very therapeutic.

6) Honor your knowing and the signs – Do not waste your valuable energy trying to convince others of your beliefs or experiences that have happened. Just as my friend shared with me about her experiences, pay attention to those who enter your life and gift you with conversations and perspective.

7) Take photos. I wrote about this extensively in another chapter in this book but I'll sum up my point with this: If I could tell every person who has just lost someone dear to them one thing it would be, "take photographs". Go into your loved one's space and take a photo of the way the reading glasses are sitting on the side table, how the spice cabinet looks, or the jacket hanging on the hook.

Photograph the wall of framed photos, the collection of ball caps or figurines. Capture the yard, the tools on a workbench in the garage, the view from the kitchen table, even their favorite chair.

In the years following my mom's death the walls were repainted, furniture replaced and passed down to us kids. Slowly my mom's decorating style and personality were taken out of the house. I am so grateful to this day of any photos I have where I can see parts of her decorating and style in the background.

This time will pass. Grip it with all you can while you are in this sacred, painful, hyper-focused emotional and mental place. There is a bond still to your loved one in your daily thoughts and activities. Even though you would never choose to be in this situation… someday you will look back and realize that this hard time was sacred.

Dream

My mum passed away very quickly and unexpectedly only a week before we were supposed to celebrate Christmas together and all the circumstances surrounding her sudden death still haunt me to this day 15 years on. I had seen her alive a year before and since she lived in Rome and I lived abroad, I never managed to see her one last time and give her comfort towards the end. In the first few months following her death, she communicated with me in various ways and experienced things that I hadn't up till then or since. I could sense that she felt torn between this reality and the spirit world and she wanted to find ways to reassure me that she was now fine and that I needn't worry. One day as my daughter and I were sat in our sun lounge, we both saw my mum, looking younger than 68 (the age she passed away) and standing in my husband's workshop curiously looking around. The previous year she had witnessed my husband building his workshop and was not surprised to see her appear there! For a few moments I felt so much happiness for seeing her again, but as soon as she vanished, again I felt intense grief and loss. In the following months, I felt her presence around the house and one night a distinct feeling that she was staring at me while I was brushing my teeth. One night as I was walking back from work and was crying almost all the time at this point, I saw this ethereal figure walking with me on my right side and felt the gentle pressure of her hand on my shoulder. 3 or 4 months after her death, I would hear her voice inside my head telling me that she felt torn between earth and heaven and wanted to give me a sign that she was ok before moving on. Soon after I had a very vivid dream of her and me in the most beautiful garden you could ever imagine, her smiling and looking happy and telling me that she was happy where she was now and not to worry about her. She looked younger and happier than she had been in a very long time, as sadly my mum struggled with depression for the last 10 years of her life. I had never seen a ghost before my mum's and nor have I since then, and this proves to me that our spirit lives on and that our loved ones watch over us all the time and that she's indeed my guardian angel.

Nicla Williams

In the
silence
my soul
hears
the
abundant
offerings
of the
universe.

–Noelle

You Are Worthy

If your loss is very recent then know that it is important to honor each stage of grief. It is important to not jump from shock and denial to diving into all I say below. It is okay to mourn, cry, scream, mope, and feel sad or angry, gift yourself grace as you work through these emotions. Save this chapter for at least a month or two after your loss, possibly longer.

Still reading? Welcome to you. I am going to tell you something that may sound insensitive at first: You are more than the person who lost someone you loved. You are more than a widow or widower, you are more than a daughter, and you are more than a mom or sister. This part of your identity may be swallowing your life whole right now but know that you are also more than that.

Your life does not stop because someone you loved so dearly is not here. You are not abandoning your deceased loved one by continuing with your life. There is a beautiful way you can give yourself permission to be sad, angry, or even lost, while also being powerful and honoring to them at the same time. Your story can continue with you using this time as a chapter marker, a pivot point. A moment you took back your inner wisdom and accept once again that life is short. What are the things you want to do or the difference you can make with others before your days are up here? Honor the loved one you lost and pick up the baton where they left off and run with it. Take their memory and all you loved about them as motivation tucked in your heart as you warrior on.

Feel your humanness. If you could talk to your loved one on the other side what would they say? I am going to assume that none of them would want them to be the reason we gave up on our own dreams and other relationships. Most likely they would tell us they love us, they are okay, they honor that we have work to do. At the end of this book are pages full of prompts that can help you piece together how you can move forward in a way that is authentic to you and also honoring all that you have been through. They can also help you find purpose for your life, for carrying on.

Finding our way forward can feel impossible at times. The uncertainty, doubts, and fears can feel impossible to work through. Keep showing up, pray for guidance and strength. Know that this is normal, you are not a failure for feeling deep. Also know that things will reveal themselves that you do not see now. Trust that your path is being laid out in front of you, there is a purpose for you and joy in your future again.

Bee Visitor

There's no school.

Which means no basketball game.

There is however an auction tonight that I could make it to.

I love the auction house and I LOVE the people there. They are part of my circle.

In my head I was debating...should I go tonight? Is it too soon?

I need and want some normalcy at least for today...

While I was in the shower, I was talking to him.

"Do you think this is okay? Doug, should I go? Is it disrespectful? Would you feel bad?

I want to be around some normalcy.....blah blah blah" I turned around and a bee was on

the shower wall!! I screamed "HELLO. OH MY GOD. HI"

I then dropped to my knees and sobbed. Uncontrolled crying. And laughter.

Uncontrolled laughter. AND then needed to document this!!

So....tonight I am going. I am going to go and laugh and maybe cry and feel

normal for a bit...and I have his blessings to do so.

Over the past year since his death, there have been dozens of bee visits.

On cue. Winter, summer, inside, outside. I savor each.

Gwen Minnick- Wright

HEAR THE
GENTLE WHISPERS
OF BELONGING
WITHIN THE
EMBRACING SILENCE

Noelle

The Path Forward

We all have a story we tell ourselves about how things unfolded with our loss, the moment we found out, how we reacted. Guilt we feel about certain interactions or previous inactions. Anger or disappointment at others. Pull yourself out of your story enough to imagine that you are watching those scenes play out in a book or a movie you are watching. Write out your story here. Claim it, release its grip on you. You can see mine laid out in the chapter, "The day" in this book, as well as pieces of each chapter in this book. (there are blank pages at the end of this book as well if needed)

My grief story:

_____

_____

_____

_____

_____

_____

_____

List 3 areas of life right now where there is a disconnect between how you are living and how you would like to be living. This could be about relationships, physical health, finances, hobbies, career, creating calm or finding more energy, boundaries with others... You get the idea. Be real, no one will see this but you and it will start to provide a road map for you to begin putting a plan in place to get from point A) where you are now to point B) where you want to be in each of these areas.

Disconnect 1:

_____

_____

_____

Disconnect 2:

_____

_____

_____

Disconnect 3:

_____

_____

_____

While putting our lives back together in a new way it can take extra focus and energy. It also can be exhilarating to finally feel like we are gaining control again over certain areas of our lives.

Plan a stress detox period and use your energy wisely when you are making big changes. Put yourself in the best possible mindset. Some things I have found to help me:

- avoid negative news and stressful movies and television
- eat real food
- avoid energy sucking people, this may require some boundaries being put in place
- get enough sleep
- cut down on social media
- good music: woman power anthems, uplifting, or whatever picks you up.

Put your blinders on. Stay out of comparison and instead focused on your own needs and growth. After big life changes or loss there are times where I heavily journaled and needed to put my actions in place to rebuild my life. Talking about it to others is not the same as actually making the changes, I needed to do the work. Writing out a plan is sometimes part of that work.

Sometimes "the work" is about cutting out things and more about starting a "stop doing" list, or eliminating contact with toxic family or friends. Pay attention to things that are sucking your precious energy and cut down or eliminate these things. It may be cutting out sugar, cigarettes, or alcohol, or maybe getting enough sleep, working out, prayer, doing a puzzle, or even taking a walk.

5 changes I can make to honor my energy:

1.

2.

3.

4.

5.

Find a support system to help you implement these changes and the 3 areas of disconnect. Is there an in-person or online support group, a coach, professional, friends, club, or tool that can help you?

Support system and accountability ideas:

Faith

I have never had my faith questioned as much as when my mom died. I had to really put my beliefs to the test. What do you believe? Have you ever questioned it, or do you follow the beliefs of your parents? Here are some questions to ask yourself to dig deeper into your own faith and how you connect to it:

1. Do you identify with a specific religion or consider yourself more spiritual? Do you find inspiration in pieces of many religions or consider yourself Agnostic, Atheist? List that here:

2. If you go to church, do you believe everything they teach? What resonates with you the most? What do you connect with the least? Is there a style of church that you identify with more than others? Quiet, small, and intimate with a deep connection to a small group of people? Or possibly a larger church with newer music and message related to real life situations. Or something else?

3. Were you brought up in your family to believe certain things? This could be a lack of spirituality or a very strict religious upbringing. Are there parts of that experience that you really do not believe in? It is important to also remember that we are all human. Do not fault an entire religion or spiritual practice based on the human mistakes people around you may have made. Have you researched the beliefs of different religions or are you basing your opinions of what others have forced on you?

4. Do you believe in the power of prayer? Have you looked up specific scripture or teachings that can be helpful to you during this time of grief?

5. Do you prefer to worship alone and have more of a one on one relationship with your creator? Or do you thrive off the energy and feeling of community by worshiping or practicing your faith in a church or other environment?

6. Are you basing your beliefs off a position of rebelling against another human? This could be for political reasons, anger towards someone you knew/know who was of a certain faith, someone within the church who acted poorly, or a power struggle within married couples. (Do not judge yourself if you identify with any of the above. Instead let us bring awareness to it. Is there a way you can find a more neutral way of viewing those areas? Are there books you can read, documentaries you can watch or ways to neutralize your feelings while learning more?

7. What do you think happens to us when we die?

8. What to do picture our creator as? Energy, God, light, a feminine and masculine pair of Gods?

It is important that we find what most rings true for us. Do not worry about what others will think. Remember, NO ONE has all the answers. No one. They call it faith for a reason. Coming up with answers is the first step in starting to clarify what YOU believe. It is a starting point, if you wish for stronger knowledge in this area you may want to read books about spirituality and faith, and various religions. You may also want to meditate, pray, and feel what is true inside of you.

Boundary setting and a stress brain dump

You are going to want to grab a sheet of paper. This process is something you can do weekly, monthly, or whenever needed. Go ahead and write down everything or person that is adding stress to your life. It can be simple things like not wanting to forget to buy cotton balls at the store on the next visit or the names of people who either intentionally or unintentionally bring drama or hurt into your life. Write down projects on your mind, goals that you have not gotten too yet, even unresolved decisions or positive things that you just have not gotten to yet that you do not want to forget. Everything you can think of that is taking up space in your brain. I first did a version of this years ago with my business coach, Christine Kane. I was so amazed at how helpful it was to unload it all and have it on paper. I have adjusted this process to work after grief or a major life changes. Once you have all your stressors down on paper, look at each one of those things. Circle the things that you cannot do anything about at this moment. These things might be a health crisis a loved one is going through, a fingernail you cut too short, or anything in between. As you look at each one of these circled items, say a prayer for them and the result. Release them in the spirit of trust and prayers for your hoped outcome or something better.

Next, put a square around any person on that list that you know is toxic. This can be someone who depletes your energy consistently without returning the help, is mean or abusive, or cannot be trusted. It does not even have to be as dramatic as those, it can simply be someone who after every encounter leaves you worse than they found you. What boundaries can you put in place with that person? Is the solution to limit contact? Or maybe it is to adjust your expectations of them so they cannot continually disappoint. Or is it someone who manipulates or genuinely makes you feel bad? Can you cut off contact with them at some level? Can you do this in a way that honors your integrity? You do not want to cut off someone out simply because you are avoiding a conversation or there was a simple disagreement, it's more of a tool for unapologetic patterns of people have that negatively affect your life. Used in that way it can be an incredibly freeing gift.

Lastly, look through the remaining items and people. Are there things that can be fixed today on that list? Simple things: folding the laundry, a phone call you have been avoiding, paying a bill, etc. Next make a list of the remaining items and work to find ways to resolve these over the next weeks and months. You have been through enough with your loss. You no longer need to carry the weight of other's lists or your own previous expectations. Adjust to life now and what makes sense as you align your goals, dreams, purpose, integrity, those around you, and the memory of your loved one(s).

Anthony Robbins talks about the six human needs. They are:

1. **Certainty**: assurance you can avoid pain and gain pleasure
2. **Uncertainty/Variety**: the need for the unknown, change, new stimuli
3. **Significance**: feeling unique, important, special, or needed
4. **Connection/Love**: a strong feeling of closeness or union with someone or something
5. **Growth**: an expansion of capacity, capability or understanding
6. **Contribution**: a sense of service and focus on helping, giving to, and supporting others

Each of us value these in different orders. When we know these areas, we can consciously look at them an analyze where we may be falling short during any given season. Go over these six areas, what order do you prioritize them in? Second, how you are meeting each need in your life right now. List them in order below and after each one write how you are meeting that need in your life:

1.

2.

3.

4.

5.

6.

Sometimes staying in drama past a healthy point helps us meet these needs as well. It can cause an increased feeling of significance or connection. If you are in a deep state of grief long after a loss, consciously analyze if you could be feeding off those needs in an unhealthy way. Is there a better way you can meet those needs that more closely aligns with your future goals?

Where do you go from here?
For some of you, major life decisions are looming. Should you sell the house? What do you do with dad's car? How can you possibly sort through a loved one's possessions and know what to do with each item?

For some the choices are obvious, others are going to require some deep reflection and honoring of your own needs. The other day I found myself talking out a problem with my husband, I was explaining what I wanted to do and why. After I finished, I realized it was almost as if I was wanting him (or anyone) to give me permission to take a bold step. It felt vulnerable to deem myself ready to take a step that others may not understand. For some of you, you may be in that same position. Newly widowed and wanting permission to sell everything and spend some time finally traveling. For someone else it may be to finally quit your job and move closer to a child. Going back to school, selling a possession of the deceased, it may just be to gift yourself a nap each day for a while. Typically, they say to wait six months to a year after a big loss. You can reach out to people you trust and have them help you weigh your options. At the end of the day though, you do not need permission! There are so many ways we can be better at honoring our needs and dreams.

Let's cover some practical steps and tools you can use to making decisions:
1. To make a decision in the first place you can use a pros and cons list, +'s and -'s. List all options out. Then under them or next to them list out all effects, feelings, possibilities that could come from that decision.
2. Go through the 10's; asking yourself "How will this affect me in 10 minutes, 10 days, 10 years?".
3. Ask yourself, is it going to hurt others? Does it align with your values, budget, honor?
4. Talk with someone you trust, have them help lay out your options and help you gain clarity.

If you decide something, then start to second guess or over-analyze; ask yourself these questions:

1. Have the circumstances changed since you made the initial decision? If yes, then make a new, educated decision. If no, then trust your first decision.

2. Does my decision align with my core values? If it does, then trust your decision. If not, then make a new, educated decision that does.

3. According to a U of Michigan Ann Arbor study, you can physically wash your hands and as you are doing it think to yourself, *I am washing my hands of worrying about this any further*. It may sound a bit far-fetched but there is data to back it up that it works.

4. Trust yourself. Have faith in your ability. Pray for guidance and peace about your decision.

5. Build your decision-making muscles. This can be as simple as deciding on a red shirt or a blue one, which car make and model you want, or making a career choice, etc. When it is the simple decisions make a note of that in your mind and give yourself the permission to make one that just feels good or will match your intention and then let it go. If it is bigger, then allow yourself some research time to make yourself more certain. Then make sure you decide. You can always make a new decision later but make sure you build your muscle in your brain that makes choices. It will start getting stronger and you will start building confidence in your decision making.

connection

Final Thoughts

You have now read all about my experience after losing my mom and others. You have read about other's experiences with losing loved ones and the signs they have been given. After reading thousands of comments in grief support groups, listening to friends, family, and reading countless books I can tell you this... The anger, frustration, devastation, and the feeling like people are rushing you to move on or you feel guilty when you have not been magically healed in 30 days... You are not alone.

I try to keep things positive and attract that energy wherever I can, but it is worth mentioning that sometimes a death brings out the worst in people. If you are on the receiving end of this, I am sending you wishes of strength, peacefulness, and the wisdom to act with integrity.

I am so honored that our paths cross. I hope that this book was able to validate and bring more clarity to understanding *Sacred Hellos* from our loved ones. I wish you all the best on your healing, grief, and future. Shine your light. The world needs you and your story, your dreams. Peace and love to you!

The following page features a grief manifesto I have created; you are welcome to cut out of this book and post for yourself to see if it resonates with you. I also have a free download on my website here: https://noellerollinsart.com/manifesto-download/

Interested in continuing the conversation on this topic? Join me online: NoelleRollinsArt.com

Grief and healing
Soulful
MANIFESTO

- I am not alone.
- I can be fully in my grief and in this moment and also have my life be bigger than this grief.
- I will show myself compassion and grace.
- I give myself permission to set boundaries with others, I give myself permission to take time right now in my life and sort through my feelings, my needs, my loss. I give myself permission to say no to those who don't have my best interest at heart or try to put an unrealistic time limit on my grief for their own convenience.
- I honor my grief and the wide range of emotions that come with it by learning more about grieving; through a book, a therapist, a trusted person in my life. I do not see myself as weak when I need help, I see myself as strong.
- I understand that I will most likely go through a time where I despise everyone around me. The world will feel like it's moved on around me or doesn't understand what I'm feeling and I will be resentful for it. I will allow the anger and sadness to move through me, I will journal about it, talk to a trusted friend, and allow it to pass without being all of me.
- I can talk about them. I can talk to the person I lost. It is healing to write about them and talk to them. Talk to them as if they are riding in the car next to me, at the chair across the table. I will aim to feel their energy around me and include them in my life.
- I will say thank you and notice the helpers. Those around me who have stepped up in large and small ways, I will take moments and sit in gratitude for these people.
- I give myself permission to grieve and heal differently than my family or those around me and to do so at the pace that fully supports my whole health.
- I deserve to be happy. Even if I don't feel it much right now, I know that long term I deserve to feel true joy again.
- I will find a way to honor this life that was lost. I will plant a tree, create a memorial, write a message or letter, pass on kindness to another. I will do something that feels right between us. No one has to know but it will help my heart to feel connected to theirs.
- I again remind myself that I am not alone. There are in-person or online groups, friends, trusted family, professionals.
- I will use this time of sadness to be reminded that our time here on Earth is limited. I will use this as motivation to reach harder for my own dreams. I will use this time to remind myself to make sure those around me know who dear they are to me.

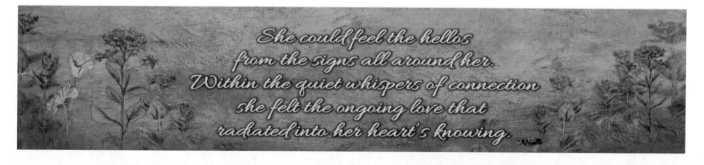

She could feel the hellos
from the signs all around her.
Within the quiet whispers of connection
she felt the ongoing love that
radiated into her heart's knowing.

Grief Resources

I share many stories in this book, my hope is through my stories you can see your own stories and find hope in them. Sometimes though, outside of the grief we are dealing with we can also have a tsunami of other life events too, multiple deaths within a short time, or we need tools and more guidance to work through putting our lives back together after a loss.

I have asked numerous groups what their best tools have been for healing after loss. Here is what they have shared with me. I have not read all of these; do not consider this an endorsement. It is more of a list of ideas so you can research and see what resonates with you and your situation. Wishing you a heart full of hope, love, and continued feeling of connection to your loved one.

- *The Grief Recovery Handbook* - by John W. James and Russell Friedman, founders of the Grief Recovery Institute.
- *The Lessons of Love: Rediscovering Our Passion for Life When It All Seems Too Hard to Take* by Melody Beattie
- *When bad things happen to good people* by Harold S. Kushner
- *Messages from Spirit: The Extraordinary Power of Oracles, Omens, and Signs* by Colette Baron-Reid
- *Angel Numbers* by Doreen Virtue
- *Your Brain at Work* by David Rock

The five stages of grief from Kubler-Ross: (note that these stages can apply to grieving a death, as well as other types of loss or change)
Denial: "This cannot be real; this can't be happening."
Anger: "Why is this happening? Who should I blame?"
Bargaining: "Make this not happen, and in return I will ____."
Depression: "I'm so sad, life will never feel good again."
Acceptance: "I'm at peace with the passing."

I was blessed to write this book and create illustrations all around the United States. This beautiful country offered inspiration, energy, and clarity.

About the Author

I am an artist and master dreamer. I see the world from a soft, loving, and soulful place.
I have been capturing the beauty of life through my art and writing, for the past 25 years.

You may be surprised by my ability to paint left-handed without leaving smears,
my obsessive love of spreadsheets, and my capability of recalling every
scene from the BBC's five-hour Pride and Prejudice movie.

After the loss of my mom, my work transitioned naturally into remembrance artwork
and portraits honoring those passed and those still with us.

I am a student of meditation, a woman of prayer and a colorful dreamer.
My husband and I are currently converting a peacock coop into a guest bunkhouse
on our property in our quaint, river town outside the Twin Cities.

Noelle

Made in the USA
Middletown, DE
06 November 2022